D1453717

KINCAID

# Touring the
# *Pennsylvania Countryside*
## *by Bicycle*

**Peter Powers**

Terragraphics ®
Eugene, Oregon

*For my favorite brothers –*
*Bill, Rich,Tom, and Dave*

## Acknowledgments

Every one of our route consultants for this book were very generous with their time and knowledge. Our thanks to Bill Kelly, George Retseck, and Bill Hoffman for sharing some great rides. And even though they *had* to because they are family, thanks to Tom, Mary, Emma, Dave, and Ujjwala for their hospitality.

Cover photo by Mel Horst, Witmer, PA

TERRAGRAPHICS
P.O. Box 1025
Eugene, Oregon 97440
(503) 343-7115

**Library of Congress Cataloging-in-Publication Data**
Powers, Peter.
Touring the Pennsylvania Countryside by Bicycle / Peter Powers, Renée Travis.
    p.    cm.
ISBN 0-944376-12-6
  1. Bicycle touring–Pennsylvania–Guidebooks. 2. Bicycle touring–New Jersey–Guidebooks. 3. Pennsylvania–Description and travel–1981–Guidebooks. 4. New Jersey–Description and travel–1981–Guidebooks. I. Travis, Renée II. Title.
GV1045.5.P4P68    1992                    92-200
796.6'4'0974461–dc20                          CIP

Manufactured in the United States of America
First Printing, 1992
1  2  3  4  5  6  7  8  9  0

# Contents

**Introduction** .............................................7

**Using This Book** ......................................9
  The area mapped. About the maps. Map
  elements.

**Resources** ...............................................13
  Maps. Books. Clubs and organizations.
  General information.

**Map Legend** .............................................17
  Key to map symbols. Map scale. Map
  orientation.

**The Maps** .................................................19
  Index map and profile comparison.
  17 street maps, 3D maps, route profile
  sets, and calorie charts. 34 route logs.

  **NEW JERSEY**
  Map 1.   Washington Crossing ..............25
           (Mercer/Somerset/Hunterdon Co.)

  Map 2.   Frenchtown ...........................33
           (Hunterdon County)

  **PENNSYLVANIA**
  Map 3.   New Hope ..............................41
           (Bucks County)

  Map 4.   Doylestown............................49
           (Bucks County)

  Map 5.   Quakertown ..........................57
           (Bucks/Lehigh Counties)
                                    (continued)

Map 6. Schwenksville .........................**65**
(Montgomery County)

Map 7. Boyertown ...............................**73**
(Berks County)

Map 8. Valley Forge ......................... **81**
(Montgomery/Chester Counties)

Map 9. Warwick Park ..........................**89**
(Chester/Berks Counties)

Map 10. Brandywine .............................**97**
(Chester County)

Map 11. Longwood ..............................**105**
(Chester County)

Map 12. Octoraro ...............................**113**
(Chester County)

Map 13. Nottingham Park .....................**121**
(Chester County)

Map 14. Amish Tour ...........................**129**
(Lancaster County)

Map 15. Witness Ride ..........................**137**
(Lancaster County)

Map 16. Hidden Amish ........................**145**
(Lancaster County)

Map 17. Lancaster Hills.......................**153**
(Lancaster/Chester Counties)

**Around Southestern Pennsylvania** .............**161**
State Park facilities. The Amish.
Weather. Places of interest.

**Cycling Information** ...................................**167**
Safety tips. Bicycle maintenance.
Equipment. Clothing. Fitness. Calorie
charts.

# Introduction

There aren't many places in the U.S. that have as dense and as extensive a network of paved country roads as does this part of Pennsylvania. If you are even a little familiar with an area this means that the variations on our routes, and the opportunities to explore beyond them, are almost endless. Remember that these are country roads – even though they are paved they are not always in the best of repair. They are also mostly narrow and without shoulders, requiring cyclists to always watch for traffic and have the skill to maintain a steady, straight line of travel.

While there are no great mountain passes to conquer in this region, neither are there routes with many miles of completely flat terrain. You will generally spend your day climbing and descending hills of various sizes and steepness. Permeating this rolling landscape is a rich cultural and historical heritage. Old mill towns along the Delaware River, Civil War Battlefields and Monuments, small farming villages, and the Amish presence in Lancaster County combine with the natural landscape of each area to present a unique cycling experience.

The influence of Philadelphia reaches quite far out into the countryside, and is felt in an increased traffic flow on roads feeding into the main arterials and freeways. The routes in this book generally lie outside the area most impacted by the growing metro area. All are within an easy reach of the city for a day ride, though some of the areas, such as those in the Amish region, lend themselves nicely to a weekend getaway.

An essential item to take along on any of these rides is a large scale county map that shows a near-complete road system with road names. The scale of the maps in this book doesn't allow us to include every road in an area. Significant roads and enough crossroads to keep you oriented are mapped, and will allow you to locate yourself on a more complete road map. Another factor in the effort to 'stay found' is the absence of road signs at every intersection. While T-intersections are easier to identify, unmarked four-way intersections can be confusing. Try to see unplanned detours as opportunites to discover the unexpected and remember that you won't have to go far to regain your bearings with a sign or landmark.

The focus of this book is its set of maps. They are as complete as they are unique. Touring, whether by foot or bicycle, throws you into an intimate relationship with the topography of a chosen route. Hills can become mountains and grades can seem to go on forever when you are under your own power. What looks like a winding country road on a typical map may actually be a series of switchbacks that climb up and over yet another ridge separating you from your destination! The 3D maps developed for this book provide you with a true representation of the landscape. The mileage log and route profile complete the picture of the ride ahead. They won't make it any easier to grind up and over those hills, but they will definitely take some of the unknown, and worry, out of your trip.

Along with the maps in this book, you'll find some general information pertinent to bicycle touring in this area. Other books cover any one of these topics in great detail. It is especially important that you become informed about fitness, with an emphasis on developing a good understanding of your capabilities and needs. Touring should be fun and fulfilling – not an unpleasant chore!

This book was designed to be taken with you as you venture around urban areas and into the countryside. The compact size is manageable for pocket or pack, and the layout will facilitate the navigation of each route.

Happy touring!

Pete Powers

# Using This Book

The addition of the third dimension to the maps in this book sets them apart from other recreation maps. The computer-generated view of the earth's surface provides valuable and clear information about the topography of an area you are planning to tour on bicycle. These 3D views accurately portray the nature of the landscape and the road system that covers it. Combined with the road map, route profile, route log, and description, they provide you with a complete picture of many of the routes to explore in this region.

## The area mapped

A good portion of southeastern Pennsylvania and western New Jersey is covered by the maps in this book. The 33 routes that are profiled in the 17 map sets are mostly loops. They include a wide range of lengths and topography, providing the opportunity for everyone to pick a route for their ability and interest.

## About the maps

While each individual map covers only a portion of the area, the entire book presents you with a picture of the whole region. Each map highlights one or two ways to navigate around a specific area. Use of the profile to evaluate hilliness and length of a route allows you to estimate how long it will take to complete it. The 3D map and road map provide the information you need to pick an alternate route or to shorten the one profiled.

The road maps are all oriented with north straight up, while the 3D maps rotate north to get the most complete view of the routes. Be aware that the scale of each map varies depending on the extent of the area being displayed.

*(continued on page 12)*

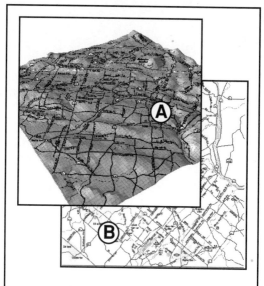

## Map elements

(A) **3D map.** This map shows the topography of the area and highlights the selected routes. It includes most of the roads and features shown on the road map, including the area's alternate bike routes.

(B) **Road map.** This is the traditional "planimetric" map, showing the route and significant roads, towns, water, geographic features, and map symbols. The mileposts along the route, as well as "direction of travel" arrows, are shown.

(C) **Route profile.** This provides a cross-sectional view of each route. Elevation lines are labeled on the left, and mileage references are indicated along the bottom. Identifiable features are located along the route to help you see where you are.

**Route logs.** This is a complete set of directions for navigating through each route. It is especially useful in weaving your way through congested urban areas. Each log shows the accumulated distance travelled between turns and identifiable intersections and landmarks.

**Index map.** *(Title page of map set.)* This small map locates the area covered by the larger maps on the following pages. It is accompanied by a general description of the area covered by the ride.

**Calorie counter.** *(End page of map set.)* This shows estimates for calories burned for cycling the mapped routes. Total calories expended over the entire loop are estimated for various average cycling speeds; the estimate doesn't take hills into account.

*(continued from page 9)*

The route profiles are displayed in a way that lets you easily compare them to each other. Don't be alarmed that some of them look more like a trip across the Himalaya Mountains than Pennsylvania topography - the vertical scale is exaggerated so that more of the "up and down" detail shows. Your first couple of rides will let your eyes and legs reach an understanding of how steep those hills really are!

We always recommend taking along a regular road map, one that shows every road in the area you are touring. It will help you get back to the route if you make a wrong turn, or find ways to extend or shorten your ride.

## Liability disclaimer

The goal of this publication from Terragraphics is to provide the most accurate and useful maps possible for Pennsylvania cyclists. The routes displayed on these maps were compiled from a variety of sources, including city, county, and state agencies and area cyclists. They are identified as being better suited for bicycle travel for safety, aesthetic, or convenience reasons. Terragraphics assumes no liability for bicyclists travelling on these suggested routes. The maps are intended to aid in the selection of routes, but do not guarantee safety upon these roads. As with cycling on any road or trail, the cyclist assumes a risk while riding these suggested routes.

# Resources

One of the attractive aspects of cycling as a participant sport is the convenience of being able to engage in it at will, be it alone or with company. However, at times you may wish for more information, or more structure, or more diversity for your bike touring. The maps in this book provide you with enough information to plan and enjoy many different rides. It is always advisable to carry along a map that has a complete inventory of streets, especially because there are so many roads in Pennsylvania and New Jersey. If deciding where to go on your next ride calls for more information for exploring unfamiliar territory, some of the following resources may help you with your planning. This is definitely not a complete list, and one of the best sources of information is always the folks at a bike shop in the area where you plan to cycle.

## Maps

*1. Specific to bicycling.*
   **Bicycle Trails in Berks Co.** Berks Co. Visitors Info. Assoc. *Three bicycle rides shown.*
   **Bicycling in Southeastern Pennsylvania.** Pa. Dept. of Transportation. *Over 200 miles of bike routes illustrated.*
   **Bicycling Suitability Map of Western New Jersey**. R. Boysen, Box 157, Califon, NJ 07830.
   **Delaware Valley Commuters Bicycle Map.** Greater Philadelphia Bicycle Coalition.
   **Hunterdon Co. Bike Trips.** Hunterdon Co. Park System. *15 routes with descriptions.*
   **Princeton Map for Bicyclists.** Princeton Twp. Clerk, 369 Witherspoon St., Princeton, NJ 08540.

2. *General road maps atlases.*
   **County maps.** Pa. Dept. of Trans.
   **Hunterdon County.** Hunterdon Co. Admin.
   **Mercer County.** Mercer Co. Engineer's Office.
   **Pa. Atlas and Gazetteer.** DeLorme
      Mapping Co.
   **Pa. County Maps.** County Maps.
   **Pa. Recreation Guide.** Pa. Dept. of Env.
      Resources.

3. *Topographic maps.*
   **USGS maps.** U.S. Dept. of Interior. *Various scales and level of detail. The 1:100,000 series is useful for planning rides of 20 - 100 miles. Can be purchased at outdoor stores.*

## Books

1. *Cycling guides.*
   **25 Bicycle Tours in Eastern Pennsylvania.**
      Backcountry Publications.
   **25 Bicycle Tours in New Jersey.**
      Backcountry Publications.
   **Bicycling in Brandywine Territory.**
      Stuart Baird.
   **Scenic Tours of Lancaster Co.**
      Lancaster Bicycle Club.
   **Short Bike Rides in Eastern Pennsylvania.**
      The Globe Pequot Press.

2. *General travel guides.*
   **Going Dutch.** Spring Garden Publications.
      *A visitor's guide to Dutch Country.*
   **Pennsylvania Trail Guide.** Dept. of Env.
      Resources, Bureau of Parks. *Identifies land and water trails in Pennsylvania.*

3. *Cycling information.*
   **Anybody's Bike Book.** Ten Speed Press. *A repair manual for do-it-yourselfers.*
   **Bike Touring: The Sierra Club Guide to Outings on Two Wheels.** Sierra Club Books. *Complete reference on bicycle equipment and touring gear.*
   **The Bicycle Touring Book: The Complete Guide to Bicycle Recreation.** Rodale Press. *Another comprehensive guide to bicycle touring.*

# Clubs and organizations

The following groups include recreation oriented, on-road cycling in their activities. There are other groups in this area that focus on racing, training, and advocating for bicycle issues.

**Berks County Bicycle Club.** 4624 Pheasant Run North, Reading, PA 19606.(215) 370-1239

**Bicycling Club of Philadelphia.** Box 30235, Philadelphia, PA 19103. (215) 440-9983

**Bicyling Federation of Pennsylvania.** 413 Appletree Rd., Camp Hill, PA 17011. (717) 761-3388

**Brandywine Bicycle Club.** Box 3162, West Chester, PA 19381.

**Bucks Co. Biking.** Box 534, New Hope, PA 18938. (215) 862-0733

**Central Bucks Bicycle Club.** Box 295, Buckingham, PA 18912. (215) 348-5679

**Cycling Enthusiasts of Delaware Valley.** 9325 Marsden St., Philadelphia, PA 19114. (215) 338-9159

**Delaware Valley Bicycle Club.** Box 274, Drexel Hill, PA 19026. (215) 789-0187

**Lancaster Bicycle Club.** Box 535,Lancaster, PA 17603-0535. (717) 656-8744

**Princeton Freewheelers** Box 1204, Princeton, NJ 08540. (609) 393-1206

# General information

**Berks Co. Visitors Info. Assoc.**
Box 6677
Reading, PA 19610
(215) 375-4085, (800) 443-6610

**Bicycle Task Force, Delaware Dept. of Trans.**
Box 778
Dover, DE 19903
(302) 736-3241

**Brandywine Valley Tourist Info. Center.**
At Longwood Gardens
Rt 1, Kennett Square, PA 19348
(800) 228-9933

**Bucks Co. Tourist Commission**
152 Swamp Rd.
Doylestown, PA 18901
(215) 345-4552

# General information
*(continued)*

**Chester Co. Tourist Bureau**
117 W. Gay St.
West Chester, PA 19380
(215) 344-6365

**Delaware Co. Convention & Tourist Bureau**
602 E. Baltimore Pike
Media, PA 19063
(215) 565-3679

**Pennsylvania Bicycle Coordinator, Dept of Trans.**
917 Transportation & Safety Bldg.
Harrisburg, PA 17120
(717) 787-5248

**Pennsylvania Dutch Conv. & Visitors Bureau**
501 Greenfield Rd.
Lancaster, PA 17601
(717) 299-8901

**Pennsylvania State Parks**
Box 1467
Harrisburg, PA 17105-1467
(717) 787-8800

**Philadelphia Conv. & Visitors Bureau**
1515 Market St. Suite 2020
Philadelphia, PA 19102
(215) 636-3300

# Map Legend

 Route 1.

Milepost for route 1.

 Route 2.

Milepost for route 2.

 Milepost marking when both routes coincide.

 Direction of travel around route. Black arrow indicates direction of travel for both routes when they coincide.

 Limited access highway (freeway).

 Hard surface road (paved).

 Water or lake.

 Creek or river.

 Park.

 Food store.

 Starting point for each ride.

| | |
|---|---|
| Hawksville | Small town or community. |
| **Princeton** | Larger town or city. |

## Map Scale

The scale of each map varies according to the amount of land covered. Refer to the scale bar to estimate distances on the street map. The 3D map is presented in perspective view - i.e., the scale gets smaller from front to back. The route profiles are displayed in a common scale in order to allow easier comparisons among all routes in the book.

## Map Orientation

Each of the road maps is oriented with north pointing towards the top of the page. The 3D maps are presented from either a southeast or southwest point of view. The north arrow on each map indicates its orientation. The 3D maps are rotated and scaled to provide the best possible view of the routes being profiled and some of the surrounding terrain.

# The Maps

There are great bicycling areas throughout the United States. The maps in this book will help you find and negotiate some of the best ones in southeastern Pennsylvania and western New Jersey. The index map on pages 20 and 21 allows you to locate rides in an area of particular interest. The numbers in circles are keyed to the numbers on the route maps throughout the book and in the table of contents. Pages 22, 23, and 24 show the profiles for all the routes detailed in this book, providing a quick way to compare their lengths and topography. The route maps contain detailed information about specific loop rides, and also show other roads that are good for cycling.

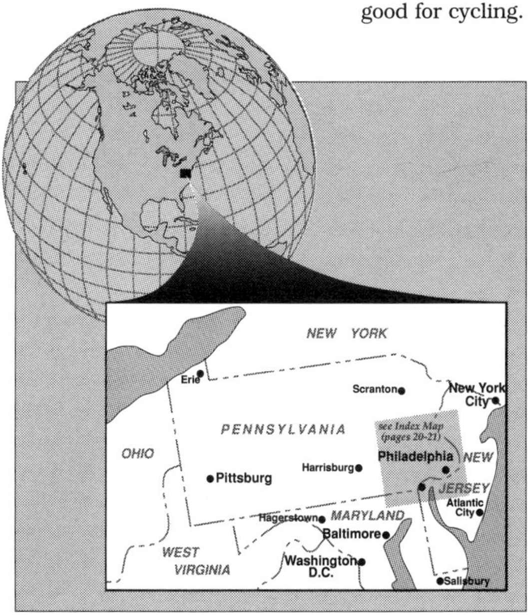

NEW YORK

Erie

Scranton

New York City

PENNSYLVANIA

see Index Map
(pages 20-21)

OHIO

Philadelphia

Pittsburg

Harrisburg

NEW

JERSEY

Atlantic City

Hagerstown

MARYLAND

Baltimore

WEST

VIRGINIA

Washington
D.C.

Salisbury

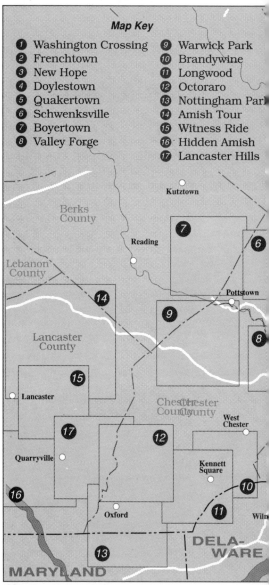

## Map Key

1. Washington Crossing
2. Frenchtown
3. New Hope
4. Doylestown
5. Quakertown
6. Schwenksville
7. Boyertown
8. Valley Forge
9. Warwick Park
10. Brandywine
11. Longwood
12. Octoraro
13. Nottingham Park
14. Amish Tour
15. Witness Ride
16. Hidden Amish
17. Lancaster Hills

Kutztown

Berks County

Reading

Lebanon County

Pottstown

Lancaster County

Lancaster

Chester County

West Chester

Quarryville

Kennett Square

Oxford

DELA-WARE

Wilm

MARYLAND

# Index Map

A key to the map sets for routes profiled in detail in this guide.

**2**

**5**

**1**

**4**

**3**

Easton

Bethlehem

ntown

Frenchtown

Flemington

Quakertown

New Hope    Lambertville

Princeton

Doylestown

Mercer County

Trenton

thampton County

Hunterdon County

Montgomery County

Bucks County

PENNSYLVANIA

Norristown

Philadelphia

Burlington County

Delaware County

N
W E
S

Camden County

NEW    JERSEY

Gloucester County

Salem County

# Profile Comparison

The profile charts on these pages and on page 24 are condensed versions of the profile charts found with each map set throughout the book. You can use these charts to make a quick comparison of the topography and length of all the routes we have covered in detail in this guide.

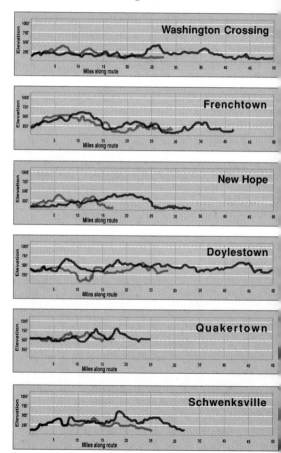

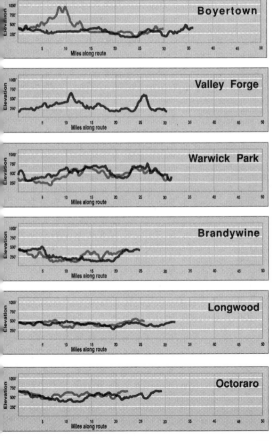

23

# Profile Comparison
*(continued)*

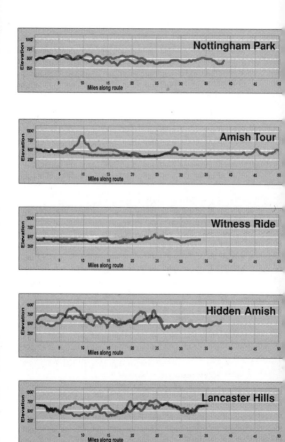

# Washington Crossing
## Princeton
### and
## Mt. Airy

These two rides start at the historic Washington Crossing State Park on the Delaware River. The park spans both sides of the river and is a great place for picnicking, relaxing and exploring after your ride. Both rides make their way through the rolling landscape of Western New Jersey before finishing with a long stretch along the Delaware River Valley floor.

Several of the towns and villages along these routes will tempt you to get off your bike and tarry *(continued on page 32)*

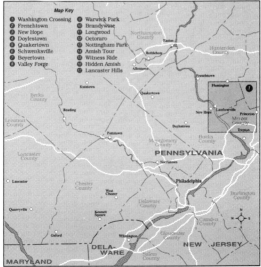

**Map Key**

| | | | |
|---|---|---|---|
| ① Washington Crossing | ⑨ Warwick Park |
| ② Frenchtown | ⑩ Brandywine |
| ③ New Hope | ⑪ Longwood |
| ④ Doylestown | ⑫ Octoraro |
| ⑤ Quakertown | ⑬ Nottingham Park |
| ⑥ Schwenksville | ⑭ Amish Tour |
| ⑦ Boyertown | ⑮ Witness Ride |
| ⑧ Valley Forge | ⑯ Hidden Amish |
| | ⑰ Lancaster Hills |

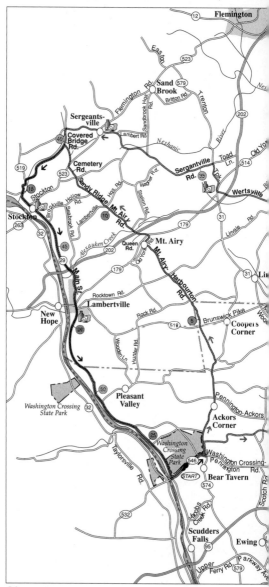

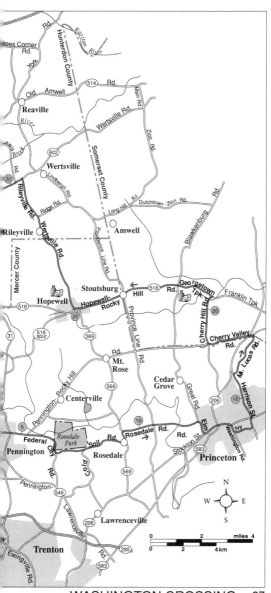

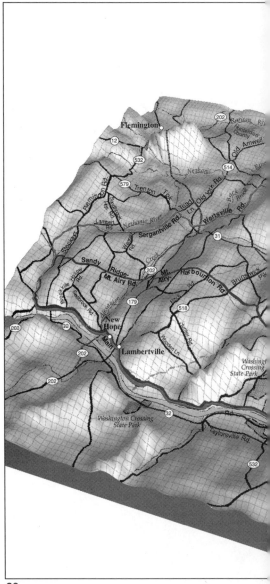

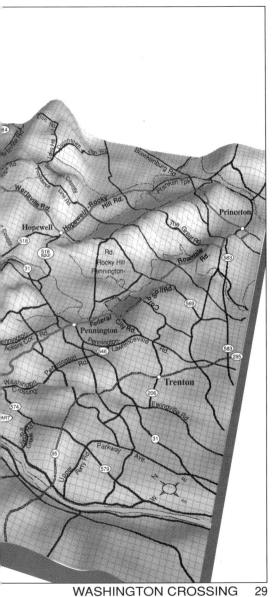

# Princeton
## 57.1 miles

| | |
|---|---|
| 0 | Start at the entrance to Washington Crossing State Park on Rt. 546; head east on Rt. 546. |
| **0.5** | **Left on Bear Tavern Rd.** (unmarked - first signal). |
| **1.0** | **Bear right, then right on Pennington - Titusville Rd.** |
| **2.8** | **Bear left at Scotch Rd.** (unmarked). |
| 3.2 | Intersect Scotch Rd./ Burd Rd. |
| 4.1 | Intersect Rt. 31. |
| 4.5 | Intersect Main St.; Pennington. |
| 5.0 | Continue south on Federal City Rd. where Rt. 624 bears left. |
| 5.8 | Intersect Old Mill Rd. |
| 6.1 | Entrance to Rosedale Park. |
| **6.4** | **Left on Blackwell Rd.** |
| **7.4** | **Left on Cold Soil Rd.** |
| **8.8** | **Left on Carter Rd.** |
| **9.2** | **Right on Rosedale Rd. (Rt. 604).** |
| 10.1 | Intersect Province Line Rd. |
| **11.7** | **Right on Elm Rd.** |
| **12.1** | **Left on Stockton St.** |
| **12.7** | **Right at intersection with Rt. 206.** |
| 13.0 | Entrance to Princeton University. |
| **13.2** | **Right on Washington Rd.** |
| **13.5** | **Left on Ivy Lane.** |
| **13.7** | **Jog right and continue past stadium;** becomes Western Way. |
| **14.2** | **Left on S. Harrison St.** |
| 14.5 | Intersect Nassau St. |
| 15.2 | Princeton Shopping Center. |
| **15.9** | **Right on Mt. Lucas Rd.** |
| **17.5** | **Left on Princeton Ave.** |
| 17.6 | Intersect Rt. 206; continue south on Cherry Valley Rd. |
| **19.1** | **Right on Cherry Hill Rd.** |
| **20.7** | **Left on Rt. 518 (Franklin Turnpike).** |
| 21.8 | Intersect Rt. 601. |
| 23.3 | Intersect Spring Hill Rd. |
| 25.0 | Hopewell Boro. |

*(cont. on page 32)*

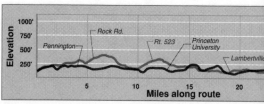

30

# Mt. Airy

## 29.4 miles

0  Start at the entrance to Washington Crossing State Park on Rt. 546; head east on Rt. 546.

**0.5  Left on Bear Tavern Rd.** (unmarked - first signal).

1.0  Intersect Pennington - Titusville Rd.

2.5  Intersect Pleasant Valley Rd. (Rt. 623).

3.4  Intersect Harbourton - Woodsville Rd.

**3.7  Left on Harbourton - Mt. Airy Rd.**

4.9  Intersect Rt. 518 (Brunswick Pike/ Lambertville - Hopewell Turnpike).

5.8  Intersect Rock Rd.

6.9  Intersect Lambertville - Rocktown Rd.

**8.2  Right on Rt. 601.**

8.5  Intersect Rt. 179; **then left on Queen Rd. (Rt. 605).**

8.9  Cross under Rt. 202.

10.3  Intersect Lambertville Headquarters Rd.

**11.6  Left on Sandy Ridge Rd.; then right on Cemetery Rd.**

**12.1  Right on Rt. 523.**

**12.2  Left on Covered Bridge Rd.**

**12.9  Left on Lower Creek Rd.;** Green Sergeants Bridge (covered bridge).

**15.0  Left on Rt. 519 (Allen Rd.).**

**15.1  Left on Rt. 29.**

15.3  Prallsville Historic District

15.7  Intersect Rt. 523; Stockton.

15.8  Intersect Bridge St.; (optional – right to find entrance to D & R Towpath).

18.1  Cross under Rt. 202.

19.2  Intersect Rt. 179 (Bridge St.); Lambertville; (optional – right to find D & R Towpath).

**26.2  Left on Rt. 546 (Washington Crossing Rd.).**

26.8  End at entrance to Park.

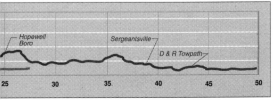

*(cont. from page 25)*
a while. Pennington and Princeton on the long ride, Mt. Airy on the short ride, Stockton and Lambertville on both routes all have retained their historic character and charm. They also offer a good choice of restaurants and food outlets.

Princeton is the largest of these towns and the campus of Princeton University makes an enjoyable side trip. In particular, the University Art Museum is worth a stop for its collections of pre-Columbian art and old master and Chinese drawings. Other campus buildings date back to the late 1700's. The town itself is full of interesting shops, restaurants, and expensive homes.

Away from the relative bustle of Princeton, these routes pass through mostly farm and forestland, with scattered housing throughout. The roads are usually narrow, two lane country roads with low traffic volume. The exceptions are found closer to the few towns, and along Rt. 29 which carries a lot of fast moving cars and trucks. The D and R Canal Towpath provides a decent alternative to cycling on Rt. 29, and is accessible in Stockton, Lambertville, and several other access points off the highway.

---

Princeton *(cont. from page 30)*
- **25.2 Right on N. Greenwood Ave.;** becomes Hopewell - Wertsville Rd., then becomes Rileyville Rd. (Rt. 607).
- 28.4 Intersect Ridge Rd.
- **29.8 Left on Rt. 602 (Wertsville Rd.).**
- 30.9 Intersect Runyon Mill Rd.
- 31.5 Intersect Rocktown Rd.
- 33.2 Intersect Rt. 202.
- **33.5 Right on John Ringo Rd.; then bear left where Old York Rd. goes right.**
- **34.4 Left on Rt. 604 (Rosemont - Ringoes Rd.).**
- 37.4 Intersect Lambertville Headquarters Rd.
- 38.1 Intersect Lambert Rd.
- 38.7 Intersect Rt. 523; Sergeantsville.
- **39.9 Left on Lower Creek Rd.;** Green Sergeants Bridge (covered bridge).
- **42.5 Left on Rt. 519 (Allen Rd.).**
- **42.7 Left on Rt. 29.**
- 43.4 Intersect Rt. 523; Stockton.
- 43.5 Intersect Bridge St.; (optional – right to find entrance to D & R Towpath).
- 45.8 Cross under Rt. 202.
- 46.9 Intersect Rt. 179 (Bridge St.); Lambertville; (optional – right to find D & R Towpath).
- **53.9 Left on Rt. 546 (Washington Crossing Rd.).**
- 54.3 End at entrance to Park.

# Frenchtown
## Flemington
### and
### Locktown

There are several quaint towns and charming villages along these two routes - and more to be found if you explore away from them. Frenchtown and Stockton are picturesque river/canal towns, with places to eat and relax. Lumberville and Pt. Pleasant on the Pennsylvania side, are quiet villages squeezed into the narrow strip of land between the river and the hills rising from it. The houses are tightly packed together, and sometimes only a few feet from the road. Flemington has a nice old downtown, and has become a center for 'factory-outlet' shopping. Quakertown, Pittstown, and Cherryville are examples of small villages that
*(continued on page 40)*

**Map Key**

1. Washington Crossing
2. Frenchtown
3. New Hope
4. Doylestown
5. Quakertown
6. Schwenksville
7. Boyertown
8. Valley Forge
9. Warwick Park
10. Brandywine
11. Longwood
12. Octoraro
13. Nottingham Park
14. Amish Tour
15. Witness Ride
16. Hidden Amish
17. Lancaster Hills

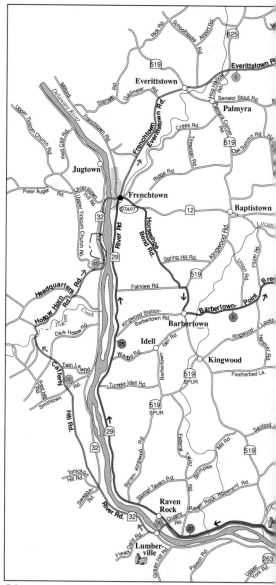

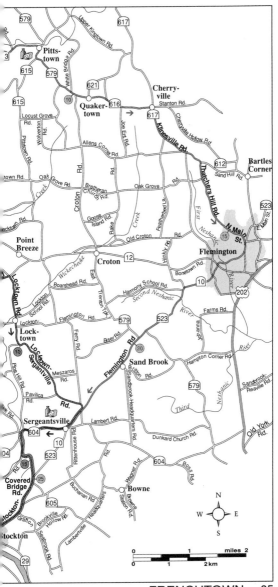

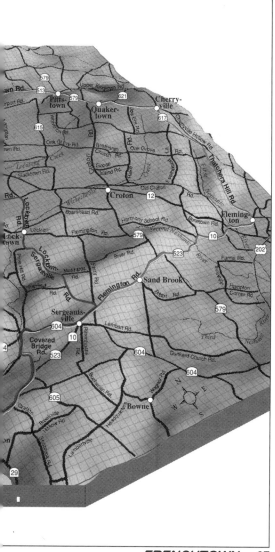

# Flemington

## 42.4 miles

| | |
|---|---|
| 0 | Start in Frenchtown at the intersection of Rt. 29 (Trenton Ave.) and Bridge St.; head north past Rt. 12 and up the hill on Rt. 513. |
| 2.7 | Intersect Gallmeier Rd. |
| 3.5 | Intersect Rt. 519; Everittstown. |
| 4.6 | Intersect Rt. 625 (Hog Hollow Rd.). |
| **7.5** | **Right on Rt. 579 (Quakertown Rd.);** Pittstown. |
| **7.8** | **Left to stay on Rt. 579.** |
| 8.4 | Intersect Quaker Hill Rd. |
| 9.2 | Continue straight onto Rt. 616 where Rt. 579 turns right; Quakertown. |
| **11.2** | **Right on Rt. 617;** Cherryville. |
| **13.2** | **Bear right to stay on Rt. 617 at intersection with Rt. 612;** becomes N. Main St. in Flemington. |
| 15.8 | Flemington. |
| **16.0** | **Right on Mine St.** |
| 16.7 | Traffic circle; continue south on Rt. 523. |
| 19.4 | Intersect Rt. 579. |
| 21.8 | Intersect Ferry Rd./Lower Ferry Rd. |
| **22.4** | **Right on Rt. 604;** Sergeantsville. |
| **23.6** | **Left on Lower Creek Rd. just before covered bridge.** |
| **24.1** | **Left on Covered Bridge Rd.** |
| **24.9** | **Right on Rt. 523.** |
| 25.0 | Intersect Rt. 605. |
| **26.8** | **Right on Rt. 29;** Stockton. |
| 27.2 | Prallsville Historic District. |
| 27.3 | Intersect Rt. 519. |
| 29.5 | Intersect Federal Twist Rd. |
| 30.0 | Intersect Quarry Rd.; **left to cross Delaware River on pedestrian bridge.** |
| **30.4** | **Right on Rt. 32;** Lumberville. |
| 32.2 | Point Pleasant. |
| **32.3** | **Right to stay on Rt. 32; go across bridge then left on Cafferty Hill Rd. in front of church.** |
| 33.5 | Entrance to Tohikan Valley Park. |
| 34.2 | Intersect Tory Rd. |

*(cont. on page 40)*

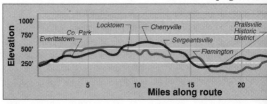

38

# Locktown

## 29.1 miles

0    Start in Frenchtown at the intersection of Rt. 29 (Trenton Ave.) and Bridge St.

**0.1    Right on Rt. 12.**

**0.8    Right on Horseshoe Bend Rd.**

2.2    Intersect Spring Hill Rd.

**3.2    Right on Rt. 519.**

**3.9    Left on Barbertown - Point Breeze Rd.**

5.4    Intersect Union Rd.

**6.2    Right to stay on Barbertown - Point Breeze Rd. where Fitzer Rd. continues straight.**

**7.2    Right on Locktown Rd.**

8.4    Locktown; becomes Locktown - Sergeantsville Rd.

9.5    Intersect Locktown - Flemington Rd.

**9.9    Left to stay on Locktown - Sergeantsville Rd. at intersection with Pine Hill Rd.**

11.7    Intersect Pavilica Rd.

**12.3    Bear right onto Ferry Rd.**

**12.5    Right on Rt. 523.**

**13.0    Right on Rt. 604;** Sergeantsville.

**14.2    Left on Lower Creek Rd. just before covered bridge.**

**14.7    Left on Covered Bridge Rd.**

**15.5    Right on Rt. 523.**

15.6    Intersect Rt. 605.

**17.4    Right on Rt. 29;** Stockton.

17.8    Prallsville Historic District.

17.9    Intersect Rt. 519 (Allen Rd.).

20.1    Intersect Federal Twist Rd.

20.6    Intersect Quarry Rd. and footbridge across river to Lumberville.

21.3    Intersect Kingwood - Byram Rd.

24.3    Intersect Warsaw Rd.

25.8    Intersect Kingwood Station - Barbertown Rd.

28.7    Becomes Trenton Ave.

29.1    End in Frenchtown at Bridge St.

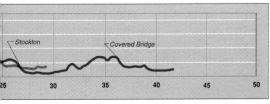

*(continued from page 33)*

no longer serve as commercial centers, but add to the visual interest and character of the countryside.

There are some good views of the river along Rt. 32, and after climbing to a ridge outside of Frenchtown you get some nice long views of the surrounding hills and valleys. Both routes cover a rolling topography, except for the flat stretches along both sides of the river. There are a few hills to exert yourself on, and a few corresponding descents to exhilarate you. At the right time of year you'll pass a number of roadside fruit and vegetable stands that might have just the right item (a juicy peach?) to refresh you.

There are Canal Towpaths on both sides of the river, though the Pennsylvania one is best suited to fat-tire bikes. Rt. 29 along here is flat and wide, with a good shoulder.

---

Flemington  *(continued from page 38)*
34.9  Intersect Smithtown Rd.
**35.4  Left at intersection with Twin Lear Rd. to stay on Cafferty Rd.**
35.9  Intersect Dark Hollow Rd.
**36.5  Right on Hollow Horn Rd.;**  Frankfield Covered Bridge (c. 1872).
**36.8  Right to stay on Hollow Horn Rd. where Cafferty Hill Rd. continues straight.**
**38.1  Right on Headquarters Rd.;  then bear left to stay on it.**
**39.0  Right at T intersection to stay on Headquarters Rd.**
**39.3  Left on River Rd. (Rt. 32).**
40.5  Erwinna.
40.7  Entrance to Tinicum Park.
**42.1  Right on Bridge St. to cross Delaware River to N.J.**
42.4  End in Frenchtown at Rt. 29.

# New Hope
## Pineville
### and
### Carversville

New Hope, the starting point for these rides, attracts a lot of visitors from nearby urban centers - especially on weekends. They come for good reason too. The town is situated on the Delaware River in a very picturesque portion of the river valley, just far enough from the influence of Philadelphia and Trenton to hold on to its small town flavor. There are good restaurants and plenty of shops to browse in, and the town itself invites you to make time for a leisurely stroll.

The surrounding countryside is a pleasant mixture of farm and forest land. Throughout *(continued on page 48)*

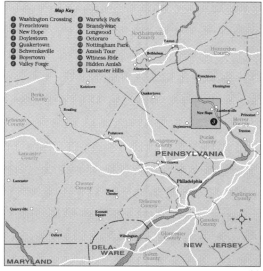

Map Key
1. Washington Crossing
2. Frenchtown
3. New Hope
4. Doylestown
5. Quakertown
6. Schwenksville
7. Boyertown
8. Valley Forge
9. Warwick Park
10. Brandywine
11. Longwood
12. Octoraro
13. Nottingham Park
14. Amish Tour
15. Witness Ride
16. Hidden Amish
17. Lancaster Hills

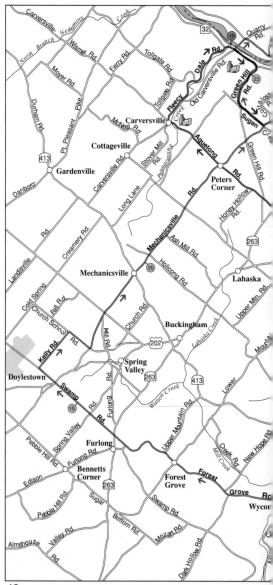

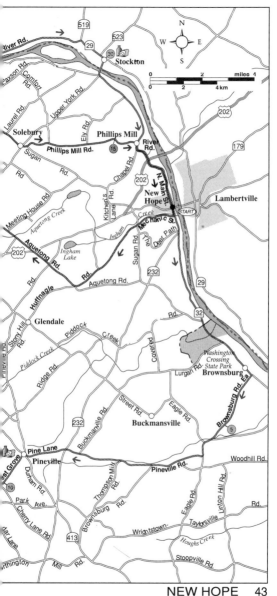

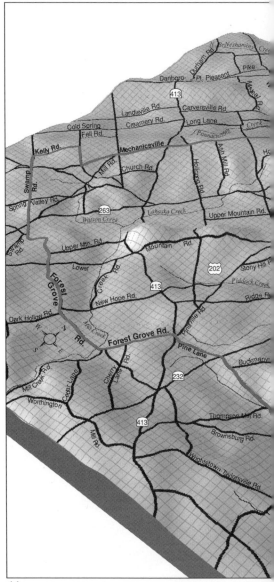

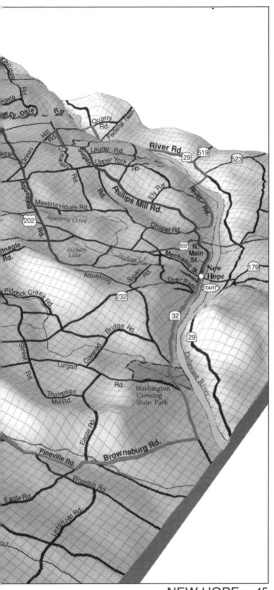

# Pineville

## 33.5 miles

| | |
|---|---|
| 0 | Begin in New Hope at the intersection of Rt. 32 (Main St.) and Rt. 179 (Bridge St.); head south on Rt. 32. |
| 0.5 | Intersect Rt. 232; becomes River Rd. |
| 2.3 | Intersect Aquetong Rd. |
| 2.4 | Entrance to Washington Crossing State Park. |
| 2.9 | Intersect Lurgan Rd. |
| **3.7** | **Right on Brownsburg Rd.** (note: watch for the road and street sign sandwiched between two houses). |
| **5.2** | **Right on Stony Brook Rd.** |
| 5.4 | Intersect Eagle Rd. |
| **5.6** | **Right on Pineville Rd.** |
| 6.7 | Intersect Brownsburg Rd. West. |
| 7.3 | Intersect Thompson Mill Rd. |
| 8.4 | Intersect Rt. 232 (Windy Bush Rd.); **cross and bear left onto Pine Lane.** |
| **9.2** | **Right on Rt. 413 (Durham Rd.); then left on Township Line Rd.; Pineville.** |
| 10.3 | Wycombe; becomes Forest Grove Rd. |
| 10.8 | Intersect Smith Rd. |
| 11.5 | Intersect New Hope Rd. |
| 12.7 | Intersect Lower Mountain Rd. |
| 13.0 | Intersect Upper Mountain Rd. |
| 13.9 | Continue straight where road bears left (unmarked). |
| 14.2 | Intersect Old York Rd.; continue straight onto Rt. 313 (Swamp Rd.) |
| 15.7 | Intersect Rt. 202. |
| **16.1** | **Right on Smoke Rd. (Kelly Rd.).** |
| **17.0** | **Right on Church School Rd.** (unmarked T-intersection). |
| **17.5** | **Left on Mechanicsville Rd.** (unmarked 4-way intersection with firehouse on left). |
| 18.2 | Intersect Burnt Hill Rd. |
| 19.2 | Intersect Rt. 413; Mechanicsville. |
| 20.8 | Intersect Street Rd. |
| 21.9 | Intersect Aquetong Rd. |
| 22.6 | Intersect Greenhill Rd. |
| **23.1** | **Left on Sugan Rd.** |
| **24.5** | **Right on Greenhill Rd.** *(cont. on page 48)* |

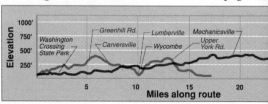

# Carversville

## 17.2 miles

| | |
|---|---|
| 0 | Begin in New Hope at the intersection of Rt. 32 (Main St.) and Rt. 179 (Bridge St.); head south on Rt. 32. |
| **0.2** | **Right on Mechanic St.** |
| **0.8** | **Bear left on Stony Hill Rd.** |
| **1.0** | **Bear left to stay on Stony Hill Rd.** |
| 1.1 | Intersect Sugan Rd. |
| **2.8** | **Right on Aquetong Rd.** |
| 3.4 | Intersect Lower Mountain Rd. |
| 3.8 | Intersect Rt. 202 (Lower York Rd.). |
| 4.3 | Intersect Upper Mountain Rd. |
| 5.1 | Intersect Upper York Rd.; **jog right and continue on Aquetong Rd.** |
| 5.4 | Intersect Greenhill Rd. |
| 6.5 | Intersect Mechanicsville Rd. |
| 7.3 | Intersect Saw Mill Rd. |
| 7.8 | Carversville; **bear right onto Fleecydale Rd.** |
| **8.3** | **Bear left at fork to stay on Fleecydale Rd.** |
| 8.9 | Intersect Fretz Mill Rd. |
| **9.9** | **Right on River Rd. (Rt. 32).** |
| 10.1 | Lumberville. |
| **10.6** | **Right on Greenhill Rd.** |
| **11.5** | **Left on Sugan Rd.** |
| 12.1 | Intersect Mechanicsville Rd.; **left to stay on Sugan Rd.** |
| **12.3** | **Bear right to stay on Sugan Rd.** |
| 12.5 | Intersect Paxson Rd. |
| 13.3 | Intersect Upper York Rd. (Rt. 263); continue straight onto Phillips Mill Rd. |
| 14.2 | Intersect School Lane (caution: watch for trucks hauling from a quarry along here). |
| **15.7** | **Right on River Rd. (Rt. 32).** |
| 16.2 | Intersect Rt. 202. |
| 17.2 | End in New Hope at Bridge St. |

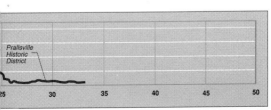

Prallsville
Historic
District

25    30    35    40    45    50

*(continued from page 41)*

the area are houses and buildings ranging from well preserved historic homes, industrial sites, and churches, to large estates and more modern development. You will be cycling through a rolling landscape, with some steeper and longer hills that drop down to the Delaware River.

Also to be found throughout this area are some old inns, either in villages like Lumberville or off by themselves. The large number of paved country roads that lace the countryside offer unlimited variations in possible routes, and many days of great exploring.

Most of the backroads around here have decent pavement and little traffic though most lack any kind of paved shoulder. Traffic moves quickly along Rt. 32, so use extra caution especially where it is narrow and winding.

---

Pineville   *(continued from page 46)*
**25.5 Left on River Rd. (Rt. 32).**
26.0 Lumberville; **right to cross Delaware River on footbridge.**
**26.4 Right on Rt. 29.**
29.2 Intersect Rt. 519 (Allen Rd.).
29.4 Prallsville Historic District.
29.9 Intersect Rt. 523; Stockton.
**30.0 Right on Bridge St.**
**30.3 Left on Rt. 32 (River Rd.).**
32.0 Intersect Phillips Mill Rd.
32.5 Intersect Rt. 202.
33.5 End in New Hope at Bridge St.

# MAP FOUR

# Doylestown
## Lake Nockamixon
### and
## Covered Bridge

Doylestown manages to combine its historic qualities with a working character to present a vital and attractive large town. There are some nice neighborhoods close in to downtown, and plenty of restaurants and food stores from which to choose supplies and refreshment. These two rides take you into an area that is less touristy than the area around New Hope. The roads are narrow and imposed on a landscape of short steep hills. Take a good, detailed street map along for these rides - there are many opportunities to miss a turn!

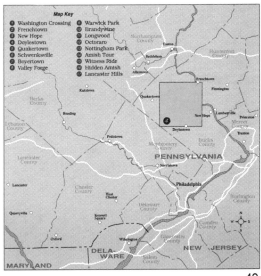

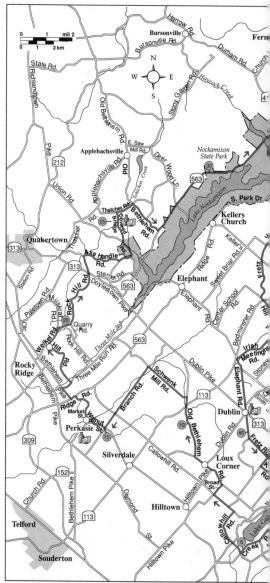

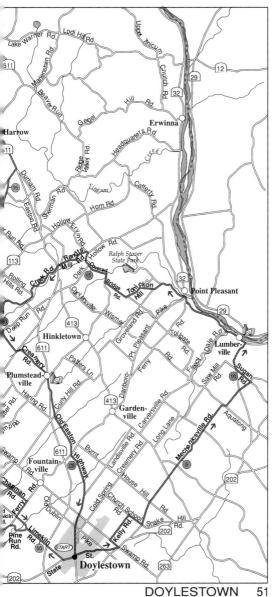

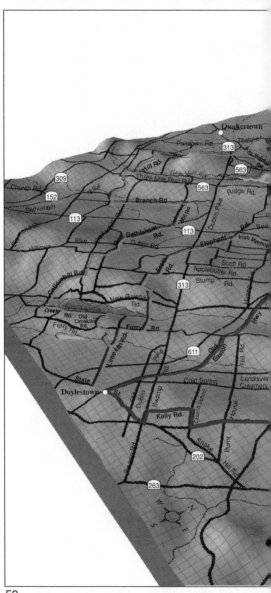

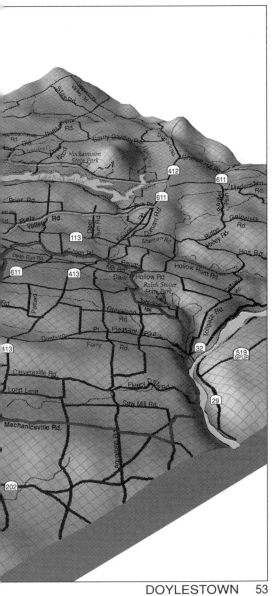

# Lake Nockamixon
## 51.7 miles

| | |
|---|---|
| 0 | Start in Doylestown at Main St. and State St.; head west on State St. |
| **0.4** | **Right on West St.** |
| 1.0 | Cross over Rt. 611 bypass; becomes Limekiln Rd. |
| **2.1** | **Left on Pine Run Rd.** |
| **2.7** | **Bear left onto Ferry Rd., then right on Old Limekiln Rd.** |
| **3.5** | **Left on Creek Rd.** |
| 4.2 | Entrance to Peace Valley Park. |
| **5.2** | **Right on Callowhill Rd.** |
| 5.7 | Entrance to Peace Valley Park. |
| **8.1** | **Right on Hilltown Pike.** |
| **8.6** | **Bear left with main road onto Upper Church Rd.** |
| 9.2 | Intersect E. Creamery Rd.; becomes Old Bethlehem Rd. |
| 9.7 | Intersect Hayhouse Rd.; continue straight where road bears left. |
| 10.7 | Intersect Rt. 113. |
| **10.9** | **Left on Schwenk Mill Rd.** |
| **12.5** | **Left on Branch Rd.** |
| **14.7** | **Right on Walnut St.** |
| **15.7** | **Right on 7th St.** |
| **15.9** | **Left on Market St.;** cross over RR tracks. |
| **16.5** | **Left on Ridge Rd.** |
| **16.7** | **Right on W. Park Ave.** |
| **17.1** | **Right on Three Mile Run.** |
| **17.5** | **Left on Hill St.** |
| **19.1** | **Right on Weikel Rd.** |
| **19.5** | **Bear left on Muskrat Rd.** |
| **19.8** | **Right on Rich Hill Rd.;** becomes Rock Hill Rd. |
| 22.0 | Intersect Rt. 313; jog left and continue straight on Axe Handle Rd. |
| **22.6** | **Right at first intersection** (still Axe Handle Rd.). |
| **23.8** | **Left on Clymer Rd.** |
| **24.2** | **Left on Richlandtown Rd.;** Weisel Youth Hostel. *(cont. on page 56)* |

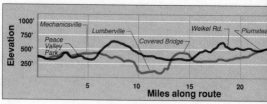

# Covered Bridge

## 28.1 miles

| | |
|---|---|
| 0 | Start in Doylestown at Main St. and State St.; head south on State St.; go 1 block, **then turn left on Oakland Ave.** |
| **0.4** | **Bear right on State St. (Rt. 202).** |
| **1.4** | **Left on Swamp Rd.** |
| **1.8** | **Right on Smoke Rd.** |
| **2.7** | **Right on Church School Rd.** (unmarked T-intersection). |
| **3.2** | **Left on Mechanicsville Rd.** (unmarked 4-way intersection with firehouse on left). |
| 3.9 | Intersect Burnt Hill Rd. |
| 4.9 | Intersect Rt. 413;  Mechanicsville. |
| 6.5 | Intersect Street Rd. |
| 7.6 | Intersect Aquetong Rd. |
| 8.3 | Intersect Greenhill Rd. |
| **8.8** | **Left on Sugan Rd.** |
| **10.2** | **Right on Greenhill Rd.** |
| **11.2** | **Left on River Rd.  (Rt. 32).** |
| 11.4 | Lumberville. |
| 11.9 | Intersect Old Ferry Rd. |
| 12.1 | Pt. Pleasant. |
| **12.2** | **Jog left, then continue straight following signs to Ralph Stover State Park where Rt. 32 turns right and crosses a bridge.** |
| 13.2 | Intersect State Park Rd. to Ralph Stover State Park. |
| **13.5** | **Bear right at intersection with Groveland Rd.** |
| 13.9 | Intersect Rodgers Rd. |
| 14.7 | Continue straight onto Covered Bridge Rd at intersection with Stump Rd. |
| **15.4** | **Right on Schlentz Hill Rd.** (T-intersection). |
| 15.6 | Covered bridge. |
| 16.2 | Continue straight onto Dark Hollow Rd. |
| **16.7** | **Left on Ervin Rd.** |
| **16.8** | **Left on Randt's Mill Rd.** |
| **17.8** | **Left on Gruver Rd.** |
| 18.0 | Intersect Rt. 611 (Easton Rd.);  continue straight onto Creek Rd. |

*(cont. on page 56)*

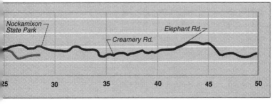

**24.9 Right on Covered Bridge Dr.**
25.4 Tohikan Campground and covered bridge.
**25.7 Right on Thatcher Rd.**
**26.3 Right on Old Bethlehem Rd.**
**27.5 Left on Rt. 563.**
28.7 Entrance to Nockamixon State Park.
**32.9 Right on Rt. 412.**
**33.4 Bear right on Rt. 611.**
**34.7 Right on Township Line Rd.**
**35.3 Left on Park Dr./Guthrie Rd.**
**35.4 Right on Park Rd.**
**35.7 Right on Creamery Rd.;** becomes Fretz
Valley Rd.
**39.4 Left on Center School Rd.**
39.5 Intersect Rt. 113; becomes Hill Rd.
**40.9 Right on Irish Meetinghouse Rd.**
**42.6 Left on Elephant Rd.**
44.3 Intersect Rt. 313; continue straight
onto Middle Rd. past Maple Ave.
**45.1 Left on Fretz Rd.**
**46.0 Right on Stump Rd.**
**46.4 Left on Keller Rd.**
**47.0 Left on King Rd.**
**47.3 Right on Chapman Rd.**
**48.8 Right on Ferry Rd.**
**49.3 Left on Limekiln Rd.**
49.6 Intersect Pine Run Rd.
50.7 Cross over Rt. 611 bypass; becomes
West St.
**51.3 Left on State St.**
51.7 End at Main St.

---

**19.2 Right to stay on Creek Rd.**
19.6 Intersect Quarry Rd.
**20.3 Left on Kellers Church Rd.**
21.3 Intersect Deep Run Rd.
22.1 Intersect Scott Rd.
**23.3 Bear right onto Rt. 611;** Plumsteadville.
**23.6 Left on Old Easton Hwy.**
24.6 Intersect Curley Hill Rd.
25.9 Intersect Point Pleasant Pike.
27.2 Intersect Landisville Rd.
27.8 Intersect Swamp Rd.
**28.0 Bear left onto N. Main St.**
29.1 End in Doylestown at State St.

# Quakertown
## Coopersburg
### and
## Sleepy Hollow

These two rides take you through rolling farm and forest landscape that exhibits little of the urban influence felt in the towns and countryside closer to Philadelphia. Quakertown has an older and charming downtown, with more ordinary and developed outskirts. There are several small, older villages, mostly without any commercial activity, scattered throughout the area – suggesting a time when the perception of daily travel distances were even more scaled down than they are when on a bike today.

Coopersburg is a simple and comfortable working
*(continued on page 64)*

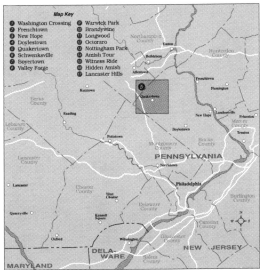

**Map Key**

1. Washington Crossing
2. Frenchtown
3. New Hope
4. Doylestown
5. Quakertown
6. Schwenksville
7. Boyertown
8. Valley Forge
9. Warwick Park
10. Brandywine
11. Longwood
12. Octoraro
13. Nottingham Park
14. Amish Tour
15. Witness Ride
16. Hidden Amish
17. Lancaster Hills

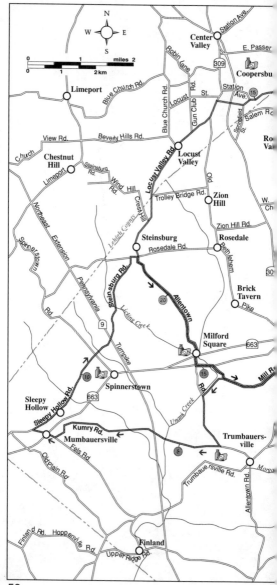

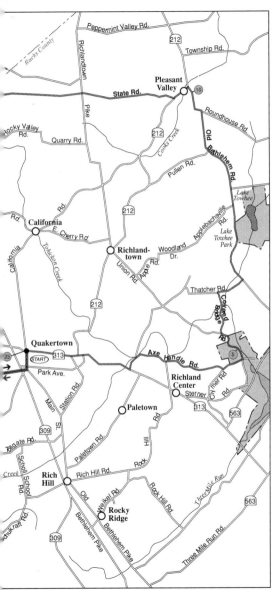

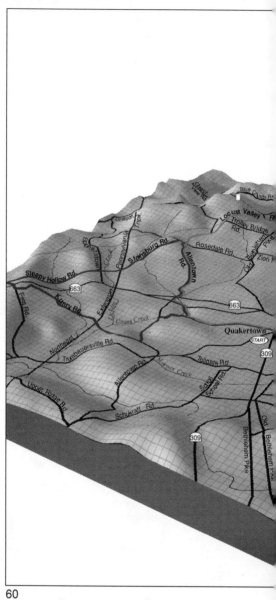

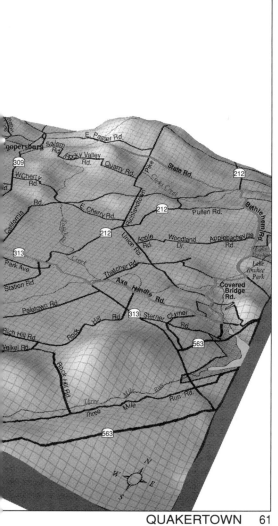

E. Passer Rd.

Coopersburg

Salem Rd.

Rocky Valley Rd.

Quarry Rd.

State Rd.

309

W. Cherry Rd.

Pike

Cooks Creek

212

Rd.

E. Cherry Rd.

Richlandtown

212

Pullen Rd.

Bethlehem Rd.

California

212

Union Rd.

Apple Rd.

Woodland Dr.

Applebachsville Rd.

Lick Run

313

Park Ave.

Thatcher Rd.

Lake Towhee Park

Station Rd.

Axe Handle Rd.

Covered Bridge Rd.

Paletown Rd.

Rock Hill Rd.

313

Sterner

Clymer Rd.

Rich Hill Rd.

563

Veikel Rd.

Rock Hill Rd.

Three

Mile

Run

Mile

Run Rd.

563

N
W        E
S

# Coopersburg
## 25 miles

| | |
|---|---|
| 0 | Start in Quakertown at Broad St. and Main St.; head east on Broad St.; becomes Rt. 313. |
| 0.8 | Intersect Front St. |
| **2.2** | **Left on Axe Handle Rd.** (at sign to Tohikan Campground). |
| 2.5 | Continue straight to stay on Axe Handle Rd. where Thatcher Rd. bears right. |
| **3.2** | **Left to stay on Axe Handle Rd.** (unmarked, three-way intersection). |
| **4.4** | **Left to stay on Clymer Rd.** |
| **4.8** | **Left on Richlandtown Rd.;** Weisel Youth Hostel. |
| **5.5** | **Right on Covered Bridge Rd.** |
| 6.0 | Tohikan Campground and covered bridge. |
| **6.3** | **Right on Thatcher Rd.** |
| **6.9** | **Left on Old Bethlehem Rd.** |
| 7.6 | Intersect Roudenbush Rd. |
| 8.0 | Entrance to Lake Towhee Park. |
| 8.7 | Intersect Saw Mill Rd. |
| 9.5 | Intersect Roundhouse Rd. |
| **10.1** | **Left on Bridge St.** |
| **10.2** | **Left on State Rd./ Quakertown Rd.** |
| **10.6** | **Bear right to stay on State Rd.** |
| 12.5 | Intersect Richlandtown Pike. |
| 12.9 | Intersect Quarry Rd. |
| 13.8 | Intersect Cut-off Rd. |
| 14.4 | Intersect Tumblebrook Rd.; becomes Station Ave. at Rt. 309. |
| **15.8** | **Left on Main St.;** Coopersburg. |
| **16.1** | **Right on Linden St.;** becomes Locust Valley Rd. |
| 17.8 | Intersect Valley View Rd.; becomes Old Allentown Rd. |
| 19.1 | Intersect Limeport Rd. |
| 19.4 | Intersect Steinsburg Rd. |
| 20.4 | Intersect Brick Tavern Rd. |
| 21.7 | Intersect Rt. 663. |
| **21.8** | **Left on Milford Square Rd.** |
| **22.2** | **Right on Hillcrest Rd.** (before airport). |

*(continued)*

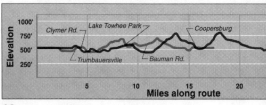

# Sleepy Hollow

## 18 miles

| | |
|---|---|
| 0 | Start at Quakertown at the intersection of Broad St. and Main St.; head south on Main St. |
| **0.4** | **Right on Mill Rd.** |
| 0.5 | Intersect West End Blvd. (Rt. 309). |
| 1.7 | Intersect Freier Rd. |
| 2.5 | Intersect Hillcrest Rd. |
| **3.0** | **Left on Allentown Rd.** |
| 4.1 | Trumbauersville; **right on Kumry Rd.** |
| 5.0 | Intersect Weisel Rd. |
| 5.6 | Cross under Rt. 9. |
| 6.6 | Intersect Canary Rd. |
| **7.8** | **Right on Fels Rd.** |
| 8.0 | Intersect Rt. 663. |
| **8.2** | **Right on Sleepy Hollow Rd.** |
| 10.1 | Intersect Spinnerstown Rd. |
| 10.6 | Cross over Rt. 9; becomes Steinsburg Rd. |
| 11.1 | Intersect Bauman Rd. |
| **12.3** | **Right to stay on Steinsberg Rd.** |
| **12.4** | **Right on Allentown Rd.** |
| 13.4 | Intersect Brick Tavern Rd. |
| 14.7 | Intersect Rt. 663. |
| **14.8** | **Left on Milford Square Rd.** |
| **15.2** | **Right on Hillcrest Rd.** (before airport). |
| **15.5** | **Left on Mill Rd.** |
| 16.3 | Intersect Freier Rd. |
| 17.5 | Intersect West End Blvd. (Rt. 309). |
| **17.6** | **Left on Main St.** |
| 18.0 | End in Quakertown at Broad St. |

---

Coopersburg *(continued)*

| | |
|---|---|
| **22.5** | **Left on Mill Rd.** |
| 23.3 | Intersect Freier Rd. |
| 24.5 | Intersect West End Blvd. (Rt. 309). |
| **24.6** | **Left on Main St.** |
| 25.0 | End in Quakertown at Broad St. |

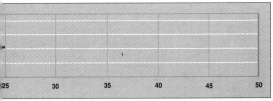

*(continued from page 57)*

town. It offers a starkly contrasting lifestyle to other small towns, like New Hope, that thrive on an infusion of people looking for an escape from the big city.

Even away from the villages and towns, the countryside is dotted with old stone and log houses and farm buildings. The roads are typical Pennsylvania backroads – paved, narrow, shoulderless, and carry little traffic.

## Notes:

_____

_____

_____

_____

_____

_____

_____

_____

_____

# Calorie Counter

## Coopersburg: 25 miles

| Average Speed (mph) | Riding Time | Calories Expended* |
|---|---|---|
| 5 | 5 hrs. 2 mins. | 690 |
| 10 | 2 hrs. 31 mins. | 760 |
| 15 | 1 hr. 41 mins. | 910 |
| 20 | 1 hr. 16 mins. | 1320 |

## Sleepy Hollow: 18 miles

| Average Speed (mph) | Riding Time | Calories Expended* |
|---|---|---|
| 5 | 3 hrs. 36 mins. | 500 |
| 10 | 1 hr. 48 mins. | 530 |
| 15 | 1 hr. 12 mins. | 650 |
| 20 | 54 mins. | 950 |

* Estimations from tractive-resistance calculations.
Whitt and Wilson, "Bicycling Science"

# Schwenksville
## Pennsburg
### and
## Green Lane

This area, north of the town of Schwenksville, includes a good mix of rolling farm land and forested hills. It has the same dense network of paved country roads found throughout the region, and the possible variations in routes are endless. And because this intense road system is coupled with a less than complete road sign program, it is good to take an 'orienteering' approach to your ventures into the countryside. Carry along a county road map to give you a more complete picture of the full road system, and pay attention to the distances between turns and intersections listed in the mileage logs. The upside of getting

*(continued on page 72)*

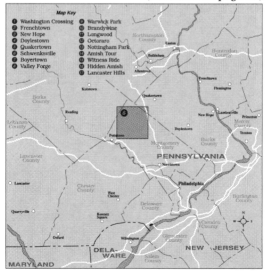

Map Key

1. Washington Crossing
2. Frenchtown
3. New Hope
4. Doylestown
5. Quakertown
6. Schwenksville
7. Boyertown
8. Valley Forge
9. Warwick Park
10. Brandywine
11. Longwood
12. Octoraro
13. Nottingham Park
14. Amish Tour
15. Witness Ride
16. Hidden Amish
17. Lancaster Hills

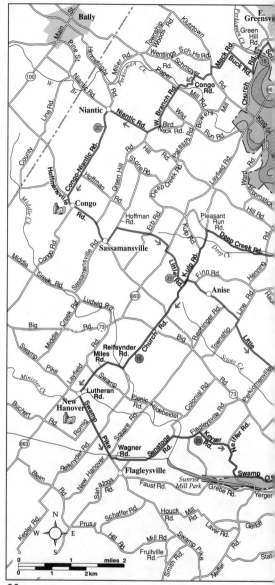

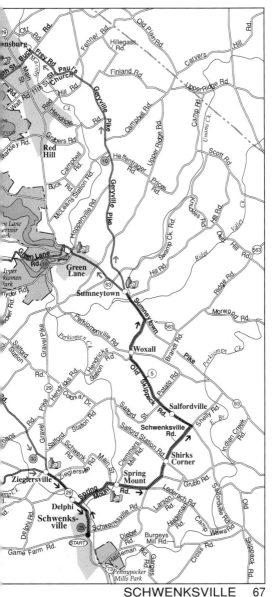

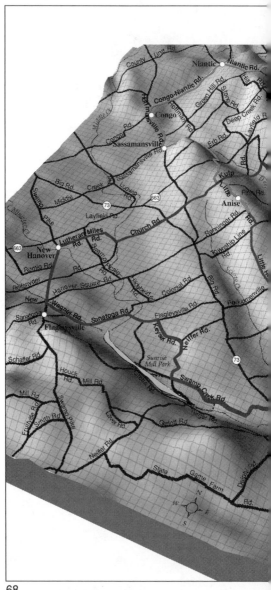

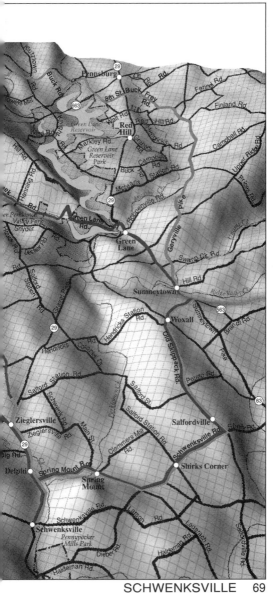

# Pennsburg

## 32 miles

0    Start in Schwenksville at the intersection of Main St. and Park Rd.; head north on Main St. (Rt. 29).

**0.7**    **Right on Spring Mount Rd.**

**1.5**    **Right at intersection with Main St. to stay on Spring Mount Rd.**

1.6    Spring Mount Ski Area.

1.8    Spring Mount Campground.

**2.2**    **Left on Schwenksville Rd.**

2.9    Intersect Salford Station Rd.

**3.8**    **Left on Old Skippack Rd.**

4.2    Intersect Wolford Rd.

4.8    Intersect Quarry Rd.

5.7    Intersect Perkiomenville Rd.

**6.4**    **Left on Sumneytown Pike (Rt. 63).**

**7.1**    **Bear right on Old Geryville Pike;** Sumneytown.

8.2    Intersect Upper Ridge Rd.

9.3    Intersect Hoppenville Rd.

10.6    Intersect Hendricks Rd.

**11.6**    **Right at intersection with Red Hill Rd.; then immediate left on St. Pauls Church Rd.**

**12.1**    **Right on Frey Rd.**

**12.8**    **Left on Buck Rd.**

13.2    Intersect Main St. (Rt. 29) in Pennsburg; becomes 8th St.

**13.7**    **Right on Montgomery Ave.**

14.0    Intersect Rt. 663; continue straight onto School House Rd.

**14.6**    **Left on Landis Rd.**

**14.8**    **Left on Church Rd.** (unmarked T-intersection).

15.0    Intersect Green Hill Rd.

**15.3**    **Right on W. Buck Rd.**

**16.0**    **Left on Mack Rd.**

**16.5**    **Left on Kutztown Rd.**

**16.7**    **Right on Schmoyer Rd.** (unmarked).

**17.0**    **Left on Congo Rd.**

*(cont. on page 72)*

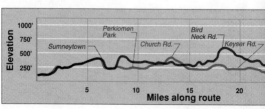

# Green Lane

## 25.2 miles

Start in Schwenksville at the intersection of Main St. and Park Rd.; head north on Main St. (Rt. 29).

**0.7** **Right on Spring Mount Rd.**
**1.5** **Right at intersection with Main St. to stay on Spring Mount Rd.**
1.6 Spring Mount Ski Area.
1.8 Spring Mount Campground.
**2.2** **Left on Schwenksville Rd.**
2.9 Intersect Salford Station Rd.
**3.8** **Left on Old Skippack Rd.**
4.2 Intersect Wolford Rd.
4.8 Intersect Quarry Rd.
5.7 Intersect Perkiomenville Rd.
**6.4** **Left on Sumneytown Pike (Rt. 63).**
7.1 Intersect Geryville Pike; Sumneytown.
**8.5** **Right on Rt. 29;** Green Lane.
**8.7** **Left at sign for Green Lane Reservoir Park.**
**8.9** **Left at sign for Upper Perkiomen Valley Park.**
9.3 Entrance to Perkiomen Park.
9.8 Intersect Creek Lane.
**9.9** **Right on Deep Creek Rd.**
10.9 Intersect Henning Rd.
11.3 Intersect Hildebrand Rd.
**12.1** **Left at Kulp Rd.**
**13.2** **Right on Church Rd.**
13.3 Intersect Little Rd.
13.5 Intersect Colflesh Rd.
13.9 Intersect Hoffmansville Rd.
14.4 Intersect Rt. 73.
15.2 Intersect New Rd.
**15.4** **Right on Reifsnyder Rd.**
**15.7** **Left on Miles Rd.**
16.0 Intersect Swamp Picnic Rd.
**16.5** **Left on Swamp Pike.**
17.4 Intersect Reifsnyder Rd.
**18.0** **Left on Wagner Rd.**
18.3 Continue straight onto Saratoga Rd.

*(cont. on page 72)*

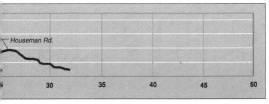

*(continued from page 65)*

lost in these areas is that it isn't hard to find your way back onto the route on paved roads – and you will probably enjoy some pleasant scenery along your detour.

---

Pennsburg *(cont. from page 70)*
17.5 Intersect Paper Mill Rd.; becomes West Branch Rd.
18.4 Intersect Bird Neck Rd.
**18.7 Right to stay on W. Branch Rd.**
**19.7 Left on Congo-Niantic Rd.**
20.1 Intersect Weller Rd.
**21.6 Left on Hoffmansville Rd.**
21.8 Intersect Congo Rd.
22.4 Intersect Green Hill Rd.
**22.9 Left on Little Rd.**
**23.3 Right to stay on Little Rd. at intersection with Hoffman Rd.**
23.9 Intersect Erb Rd.
24.5 Intersect Rt. 663.
**25.3 Left on Church Rd.**
**25.4 Right to follow main road at intersection with Kulp Rd.; becomes Little Rd.**
25.8 Intersect Houseman Rd.
**26.6 Right on Township Line Rd.**
**26.8 Left on Little Rd.**
27.5 Intersect Schweisfort Rd.
27.9 Intersect Perkiomenville Rd.
29.5 Intersect Simmons Rd.
**30.2 Bear right onto Rt. 29 (Gravel Pike).**
30.4 Intersect Rt. 73.
31.3 Intersect Spring Mount Rd.
32.0 End in Schwenksville.

---

Green Lane *(cont. from page 71)*
**19.3 Bear right at intersection with Colonial Rd.; becomes Fagleysville Rd.**
**19.8 Right on Keyser Rd.**
**20.5 Right on Neiffer Rd. (unmarked T-intersection).**
**21.4 Left on Swamp Cr. Rd.**
**23.2 Right on Rt. 73.**
**23.8 Bear right on Rt. 29.**
24.6 Intersect Spring Mount Rd.
25.2 End in Schwenksville.

# Boyertown
## Daniel Boone
### and
## Landis Store

These two rides explore a very pretty part of Berks County's farm lands. The area is far enough from the influence of Philadelphia to be still holding on to its agricultural roots. The light green fields of crops and grass open up views of surrounding hills covered with a darker green canopy. Dairy and crop farms share pleasant valley bottoms with meandering rivers and creeks, while the intervening hills provide a few good workouts for the cyclist.

The towns in here are more 'working' quaint than 'tourist' quaint. Several small villages without a
*(continued on page 80)*

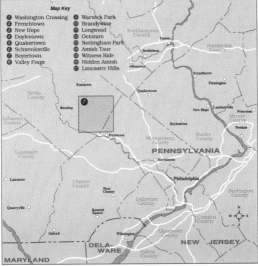

Map Key

1. Washington Crossing
2. Frenchtown
3. New Hope
4. Doylestown
5. Quakertown
6. Schwenksville
7. Boyertown
8. Valley Forge
9. Warwick Park
10. Brandywine
11. Longwood
12. Octoraro
13. Nottingham Park
14. Amish Tour
15. Witness Ride
16. Hidden Amish
17. Lancaster Hills

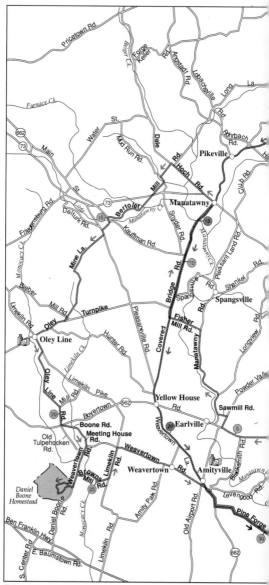

74

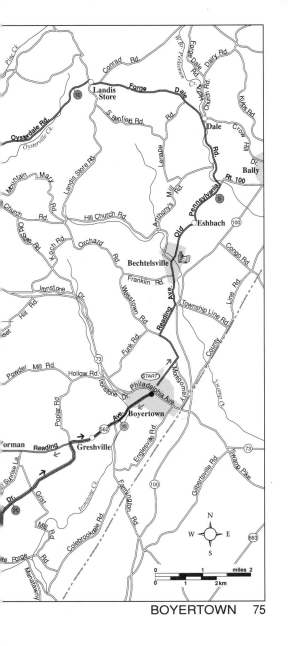

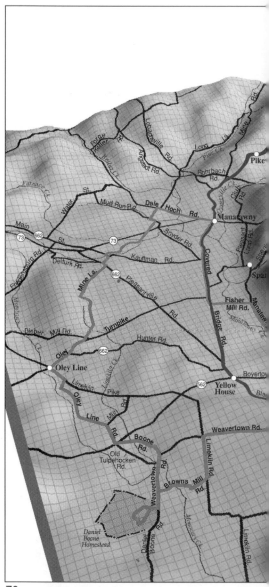

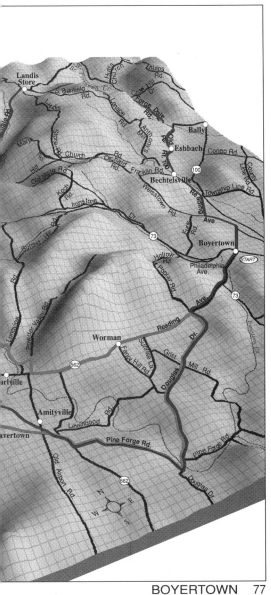

# Daniel Boone

## 36.1 miles

| | |
|---|---|
| 0 | Start in Boyertown at the intersection of Philadelphia Ave. and Reading Ave.; head southwest on Reading Ave. (Rt. 562). |
| 2.1 | Intersect Douglas Rd. |
| 4.2 | Intersect Worman Rd. |
| 4.8 | Intersect Blacksmith Rd. |
| **5.5** | **Right on Powder Valley Rd. at sign to Gablesville.** |
| **5.8** | **Left on Saw Mill Rd.** |
| **6.0** | **Right on Longview Rd.** (unmarked T-intersection). |
| **6.4** | **Bear left onto Manatawny Rd.** |
| 7.1 | Intersect Park Rd. |
| **8.0** | **Left on Fisher Mill Rd.** |
| **8.7** | **Right on Covered Bridge Rd.** |
| 9.0 | Intersect Oley Turnpike. |
| 10.1 | Intersect Kauffman Rd. |
| 10.9 | Covered bridge; intersect Toll House Rd. |
| **11.4** | **Left on Rt. 73 in Manatawny.** |
| **11.6** | **Bear right onto Dale Hoch Rd.** (unmarked). |
| **12.6** | **Left on Bertolet Mill Rd.** |
| 13.0 | Intersect Mud Run Rd. |
| 13.3 | Intersect Rt. 73. |
| **14.5** | **Left at intersection with Main St. to stay on Bertolet Mill Rd.** |
| **14.6** | **Right to stay on Bertolet Mill Rd.** |
| **14.9** | **Left on Rt. 662.** |
| **15.0** | **Right on Mine Lane.** |
| 17.2 | Intersect Bieber Mill Rd.; **bear right onto Oley Turnpike.** |
| **17.9** | **Left on Limekiln Rd.;** Limekiln. |
| **18.3** | **Right on Oley Line Rd.** |
| **19.2** | **Left on Loder Rd.** |
| 20.0 | Cross Rt. 562; **then immediate left on Boone Rd.** |
| **20.6** | **Right on Meeting House Rd.** |
| **20.8** | **Right on Weavertown Rd.** |
| 20.9 | Continue straight at intersection. |
| 21.4 | Intersect Browns Mill Rd. |
| 21.6 | Becomes Daniel Boone Rd. |

*(cont. on page 80)*

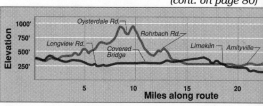

# Landis Store

## 30 miles

| | |
|---|---|
| 0 | Start in Boyertown at the intersection of Philadelphia Ave. and Reading Ave.; head northeast on Reading Ave. (Rt. 562). |
| **0.9** | **Left to stay on Reading Ave. just before Rt. 100.** |
| **1.5** | **Right to stay on Reading Ave. at Weisstown Rd.** |
| 3.2 | Bechtelsville; **bear right onto Main St.;** becomes Old Pennsylvania Rt. 100. |
| 4.0 | Intersect Robin Hill Rd. |
| **5.1** | **Left on Forge Dale Rd.** |
| 5.7 | Intersect Anthony's Mill Rd. |
| 6.6 | Intersect Huffs Church Rd. |
| 7.6 | Intersect Kemp Rd. |
| **9.3** | **Left on Oysterdale Rd.** |
| 10.6 | Intersect Rolling Rock Rd. |
| 11.8 | Intersect Hartline Rd. |
| 13.0 | Intersect Rohrbach Rd. |
| **13.8** | **Bear left at intersection with Clearer Rd.** |
| 14.6 | Intersect Rt. 73; continue straight onto Covered Bridge Rd. |
| 15.0 | Covered bridge. |
| 15.8 | Intersect Kauffman Rd. |
| 16.2 | Intersect Church Rd. |
| 17.0 | Intersect Oley Turnpike. |
| 17.2 | Intersect Fisher Mill Rd. |
| **18.7** | **Bear left onto Rt. 662.** |
| 19.1 | Intersect Rt. 562. |
| 20.9 | Intersect Old Airport Rd.; Amityville. |
| 21.2 | Intersect Weavertown Rd. |
| **21.6** | **Left on Pine Forge Rd.** |
| **23.3** | **Left on Douglas Dr.** |
| 24.2 | Intersect Glendale Rd. |
| 25.4 | Intersect Grist Mill Rd. |
| **27.9** | **Right on Rt. 562.** |
| 30.0 | End in Boyertown. |

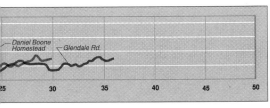

*(continued from page 73)*

commercial center dot the landscape and historic farm, residential, and commercial buildings add to the already pleasing natural landscape. The Daniel Boone Homestead gives you a good sense of what the area looked like many years ago, both physically and culturally. The visitors center is a good place to browse, relax, picnic, refill water bottles, and find a restroom.

---

Daniel Boone *(cont. from page 78)*
22.3 Entrance to Daniel Boone Homestead; follow loop through park.
23.7 Leave Daniel Boone Homestead; **left on Daniel Boone Rd.**
**24.6 Right on Browns Mill Rd.**
**25.4 Left on Limekiln Rd.**
**26.1 Right on Weavertown Rd.**
27.5 Intersect Geiger Rd.
**28.3 Right on Rt. 662;** Amityville.
**28.7 Left on Pine Forge Rd.**
**30.4 Left on Douglas Dr.**
31.3 Intersect Glendale Rd.
32.5 Intersect Grist Mill Rd.
**34.0 Right on Rt. 562.**
36.1 End in Boyertown.

# Calorie Counter

**Daniel Boone: 36.1 miles**

| Average Speed (mph) | Riding Time | Calories Expended* |
|---|---|---|
| 5 | 7 hrs. 13 mins. | 1020 |
| 10 | 3 hrs. 37 mins. | 1140 |
| 15 | 2 hrs. 24 mins. | 1440 |
| 20 | 1 hr. 48 mins. | 1970 |

**Landis Store: 30 miles**

| Average Speed (mph) | Riding Time | Calories Expended* |
|---|---|---|
| 5 | 6 hrs. | 830 |
| 10 | 3 hrs. | 900 |
| 15 | 2 hrs. | 1070 |
| 20 | 1 hr. 30 mins. | 1570 |

\* Estimations from tractive-resistance calculations, Whitt and Wilson, "Bicycling Science"

# MAP EIGHT

# Valley Forge

## Yellow Springs

Valley Forge National Historic Park occupies the site of the Continental Army's encampment during the winter of 1777-1778. We have profiled one route that starts near the visitor center and explores the countryside north and west of the Park. Because of the proximity to Philadelphia, there is more traffic and development in this area, and cyclists should be expecially cautious on the short stretches of Rt. 23.

There are several miles of roads and bike paths that connect historic sites and buildings scattered throughout the Park. A detailed 3D map of the

*(continued on page 88)*

**Map Key**

1. Washington Crossing
2. Frenchtown
3. New Hope
4. Doylestown
5. Quakertown
6. Schwenksville
7. Boyertown
8. Valley Forge
9. Warwick Park
10. Brandywine
11. Longwood
12. Octoraro
13. Nottingham Park
14. Amish Tour
15. Witness Ride
16. Hidden Amish
17. Lancaster Hills

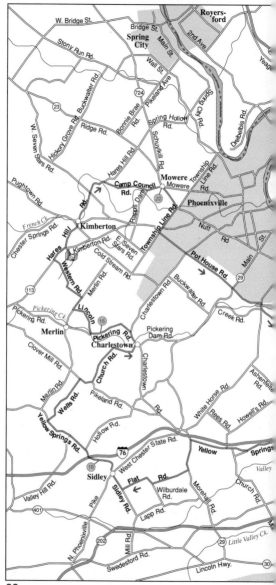

82

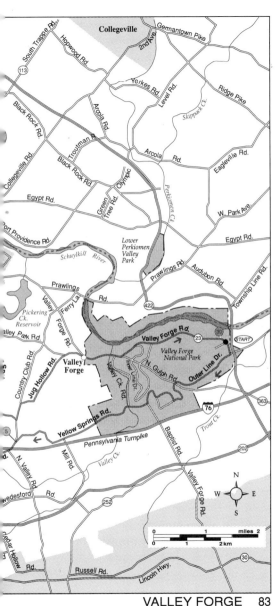

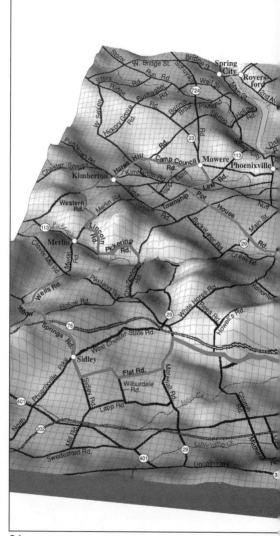

# Yellow Springs
## 30.3 miles

| | |
|---|---|
| 0 | Start at the intersection of Rt. 23 and County Line Rd. on the bike path;  head south on the bike path. |
| **0.3** | **Right on bike path to follow Outer Line Dr.** |
| 1.2 | Intersect N. Gulph Rd. |
| 2.2 | Junction with bike path that heads north to Artillery Park;  **keep left to follow Outer Line Dr.** |
| **2.6** | **Right on Valley Creek Rd.** |
| **2.8** | **Left on Yellow Springs Rd. to cross covered bridge.** |
| 3.4 | Leave National Park. |
| 5.2 | Cross under Hwy. 76;  intersect N. Valley Rd. |
| 6.6 | Intersect Church Rd. |
| **7.4** | **Left on Hwy. 29.** |
| **8.0** | **Right on Flat Rd.** |
| 8.7 | Intersect Wilburdale Rd. |
| **9.3** | **Right on Sidley Rd.** |
| 9.7 | Intersect Phoenixville Pike;  continue straight onto Yellow Springs Rd. |
| 10.3 | Cross over Hwy. 76. |
| 10.8 | Intersect Valley Hill Rd. |
| **11.4** | **Right on Wells Rd.** |
| **12.4** | **Right on Church Rd.** (unmarked T-intersection). |
| **12.6** | **Left on Church Rd.** |
| **14.0** | **Left on Charlestown Rd.** (unmarked T-intersection). |
| 14.3 | Straight onto Pickering Rd. where Charlestown bears right. |
| **15.2** | **Bear right just before bridge onto Lincoln Rd.** |
| **15.8** | **Right on Merlin Rd.** |
| **16.1** | **Left on Western Rd.** |
| **17.0** | **Right on Rt. 113.** |
| **17.3** | **Left on Hares Hill Rd.** |
| 17.8 | Intersect Kimberton Rd. |
| 18.4 | Intersect Seven Stars Rd. |
| **18.8** | **Right on Camp Council Rd.** |
| **19.6** | **Left to stay on Camp Council Rd.** |

*(continued)*

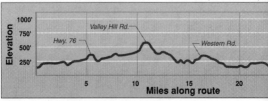

*(continued)*

**20.0 Right on Rt. 23.**
**20.5 Right on Township Line Rd.**
20.9 Intersect Rt. 113.
**21.0 Left on Pot House Rd.**
21.6 Intersect Charlestown Rd.
22.7 Intersect Rt. 29.
**23.3 Right on White Horse Rd.**
**23.4 Left on Valley Park Rd.**
23.7 Continue straight onto Clothier Spring
Rd. where Valley Park Rd. bears left.
**25.1 Bear left to stay on Clothier Spring Rd.
at intersection with Ashenfelter Rd.**
**25.7 Left on Country Club Rd.**
**26.0 Right on Jug Hollow Rd.**
**27.3 Right at intersection with Valley Park Rd.
to stay on Jug Hollow Rd.**
**27.6 Right on Valley Forge Rd. (Rt. 23).**
28.2 Intersect Rt. 252.
**28.4 Bear left on Rt. 23.**
28.5 Entrance to Washington's Headquarters;
**pick up bike path on left.**
29.1 Cross Rt. 23; stay on bike path that follows
Rt. 23.
30.3 End at the intersection with County Line Rd.

*Note: The bike paths of Valley Forge National
Historic Park are shown in detail on pages 164 &
165.*

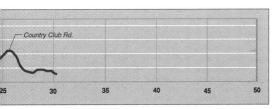

*(continued from page 81)*

Park is presented on pages 164 and 165, and more information is available from the National Park Service. You might begin your day at the visitor center, where films and exhibits can give you an overview of the history of the encampment as well as an orientation to the remains and reconstructions of the Park's forts and buildings. Bicycle rentals are available, and there are numerous picnicking sites along the bike paths. It all adds up to a great place for a family ride.

## Notes:

## Calorie Counter

Yellow Springs: 30.3 miles

| Average Speed (mph) | Riding Time | Calories Expended* |
|---|---|---|
| 5 | 6 hrs. 3 mins. | 840 |
| 10 | 3 hrs. 2 mins. | 910 |
| 15 | 2 hrs. 1 mins. | 1090 |
| 20 | 1 hr. 30 mins. | 1580 |

* Estimations from tractive-resistance calculations, Whitt and Wilson, "Bicycling Science"

# Warwick Park

## French Creek
### and
## Nantmeal

These rides were put together by the Brandywine Bicycle Club. Each is one-half of a metric century (62.1 miles; 100km). The southern half of the ride, the Nantmeal route, is somewhat less hilly than the northern half, and has fewer stores and points of interest. Warwick Park makes a good start and end point, and a picnicking spot for lunch if you attempt the full century.

French Creek State Park covers 7000 acres. It offers a wide variety of facilities and activities, including picnicking, swimming, fishing, boating, *(continued on page 96)*

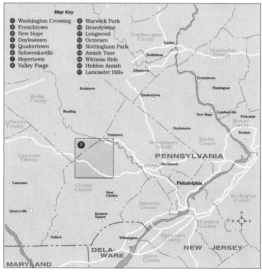

**Map Key**

1. Washington Crossing
2. Frenchtown
3. New Hope
4. Doylestown
5. Quakertown
6. Schwenksville
7. Boyertown
8. Valley Forge
9. Warwick Park
10. Brandywine
11. Longwood
12. Octoraro
13. Nottingham Park
14. Amish Tour
15. Witness Ride
16. Hidden Amish
17. Lancaster Hills

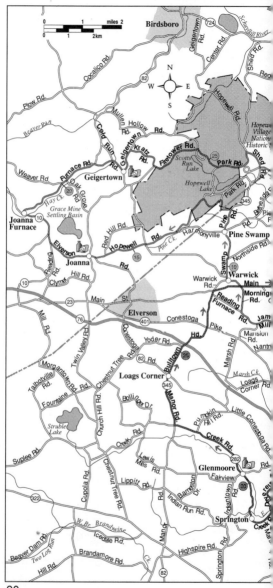

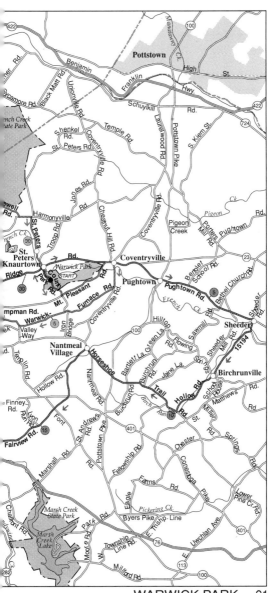

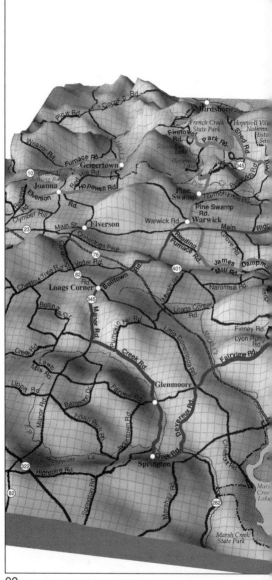

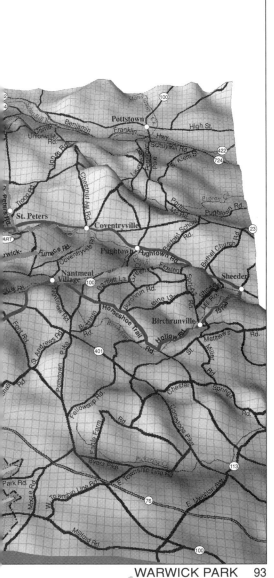

# French Creek

## 31.3 miles

| | |
|---|---|
| 0 | Start at the entrance to Warwick Park; head south on County Park Rd. |
| **0.6** | **Left on Mt. Pleasant Rd.** |
| 2.1 | Cross Rt. 23 **then right at T-intersection**; cross small stone bridge. |
| 2.4 | Coventryville; **right on Coventryville Rd. after United Methodist Church;** cross Rt. 23. |
| **3.0** | **Right on Warwick Furnace Rd.** |
| **4.5** | **Right at intersection with Iron Bridge Rd. to stay on Warwick Furnace Rd.** |
| 4.6 | Intersect County Park Rd. |
| **6.4** | **Bear left at Y-intersection (Dampman Rd.)** |
| **6.8** | **Left on Grove Rd.** |
| **7.0** | **Right at James Mill Rd.** |
| **7.7** | **Bear right onto Reading Furnace Rd.** |
| **8.3** | **Right at Morningside Rd.** (stop sign). |
| 9.0 | Intersect Rt. 23. |
| 9.1 | Warwick; **left on Warwick Rd.** |
| **9.5** | **Right on Rt. 345 (Pine Swamp Rd.).** |
| 10.8 | Intersect Harmonyville Rd.; **jog right then left.** |
| **11.4** | **Left on French Creek State Park away from direction sign to "Hopewell Village Entrance".** |
| **12.5** | **Left on Park Rd.;** becomes Hopewell Rd. |
| 14.9 | Intersect Cold Run Rd. |
| **16.1** | **Bear right onto Rt. 82;** then continue straight onto Elverson Rd. at intersection with Twin Valley Rd. |
| 16.6 | Joanna. |
| **17.4** | **Right on Rt. 10.** |
| 18.4 | Joanna Furnace; **right on Furnace Rd.** |
| **20.0** | **Left at T-intersection towards Birdsboro.** |
| **20.9** | **Right on Chapel Rd. away from Birdsboro.** |
| **21.4** | **Right on Rt. 82.** |
| 21.8 | Geigertown; **left on Geigertown Rd.** |
| **22.4** | **Right on Kratz Rd.** |
| **23.3** | **Left on Firetower Rd.; bear left at Hopewell Firetower sign.** |

*(cont. on page 96)*

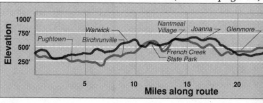

# Nantmeal

## 30.8 miles

0     Start at the entrance to Warwick Park;  head north on County Park Rd.

**0.3**   **Right on Rt. 23.**

**2.9**   **Right on Pughtown Rd.**

3.6   Pughtown;  cross Rt. 100.

**5.3**   **Right on County Rt. 15194** (at Dressed Beef Co.);  cross covered bridge over French Creek.

**8.1**   **Bear right at intersection with School House Rd.**

8.3   Birchrunville;  continue straight on Hollow Rd.

**9.5**   **Right on Horseshoe Trail Rd.** (T-intersection).

10.6  Continue straight at stop sign.

11.1  Intersect with Bartlett Lane;  continue straight.

11.5  Cross Rt. 100;  **jog right.**

12.4  Continue straight at stop sign.

12.6  Nantmeal Village;  **sharp left on Fairview Rd.**

14.1  Intersect Rt. 401.

17.3  Fairview Church;  **bear right to stay on Fairview Rd.;  then left on Devereux Rd. just past church.**

**18.7**  **Right on Rt. 282 (Creek Rd.).**

20.5  Glenmoore.

**23.0**  **Right on Rt. 82.**

24.4  Loags Corner;  continue straight onto Rt. 345.

26.1  Intersect Rd. 401.

**27.1**  **Right on Rt. 23.**

30.5  Knauertown;  **right on County Park Rd. towards Warwick Park.**

30.8  End at Warwick Park.

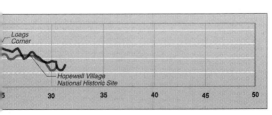

*(continued from page 89)*

and hiking. There are 260 campsites and even a few cabins for rent. Right next to the park is Hopewell Village National Historic site - a restored ironmaking village with anthracite furnace and related machinery, structures and buildings (c. 1771-1883).

St. Peters, also on the northern route, is an historic town next to the rapids of French Creek. You'll find shops, restaurants and restrooms along with the pedestrians and traffic.

---

French Creek  *(cont. from page 94)*

    **Scotts Run Lake and park office.**
24.9  Continue straight, avoiding one-way road.
**25.4  Left at Group Camp No. 2** (stop sign);
    **bear right at Brush Hill.**
**26.5  Right on Rt. 345.**
27.2  Hopewell Village National Historic Site;
    **left on Hopewell Rd. towards St. Peters.**
**29.3  Bear left onto Harmonyville Rd.**
**29.5  Right towards St. Peters on St. Peters Rd.**
30.9  Knauertown;  **left on Rt. 23 then right**
    **on County Park Rd.**
31.3  End at Warwick Park.

---

# Calorie Counter

**French Creek: 31.3 miles**

| Average Speed (mph) | Riding Time | Calories Expended* |
| --- | --- | --- |
| 5 | 6 hrs. 16 mins. | 870 |
| 10 | 3 hrs. 8 mins. | 940 |
| 15 | 2 hrs. 5 mins. | 1120 |
| 20 | 1 hr. 34 mins. | 1640 |

**Nantmeal: 30.8 miles**

| Average Speed (mph) | Riding Time | Calories Expended* |
| --- | --- | --- |
| 5 | 6 hrs. 10 mins. | 850 |
| 10 | 3 hrs. 5 mins. | 920 |
| 15 | 2 hrs. 3 mins. | 1100 |
| 20 | 1 hr. 32 mins. | 1610 |

\* Estimations from tractive-resistance calculations,
Whitt and Wilson, "Bicycling Science"

# Brandywine
## Wawaset
### and
## Delaware

These two rides start near the entrance to Longwood Gardens, the site of hundreds of acres of outdoor and 20 indoor conservatories. Other historic sites and museums attest to the area's rich cultural heritage. A dense network of roads and lanes offer many variations to the routes presented here. They can also present a challenge when you are trying to follow a route with many unsigned intersections, so be sure to carry along a map that shows the complete road system.

Both of these loops follow sections of Brandywine Creek, a pleasant stream with two branches that *(continued on page 104)*

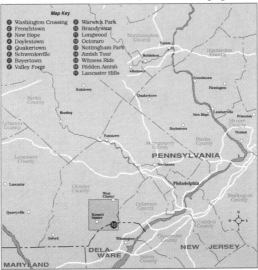

Map Key

1. Washington Crossing
2. Frenchtown
3. New Hope
4. Doylestown
5. Quakertown
6. Schwenksville
7. Boyertown
8. Valley Forge
9. Warwick Park
10. Brandywine
11. Longwood
12. Octoraro
13. Nottingham Park
14. Amish Tour
15. Witness Ride
16. Hidden Amish
17. Lancaster Hills

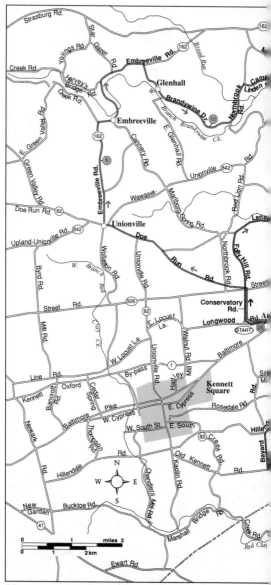

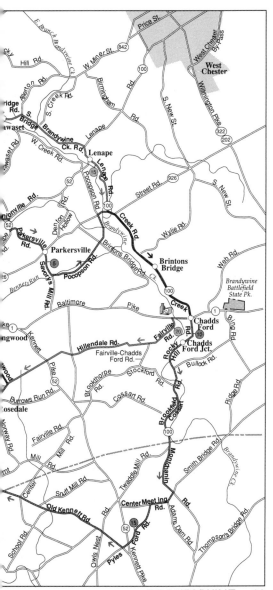

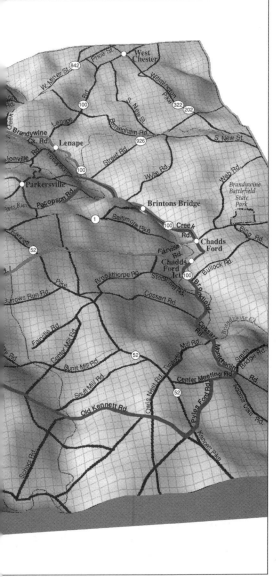

# Wawaset

## 25.3 miles

0    Start at the parking lot and picnic area on Longwood Rd. just west of the entrance to Longwood Gardens; head west on Longwood Rd.

**0.2**    **Right on Conservatory Rd.**

0.8    Intersect Rt. 926; **cross over and bear left onto Doe Run Rd.**

2.6    Intersect Unionville - Lanape Rd.

**3.2**    **Bear right onto Rt. 82.**

3.8    Intersect Rt. 842.

**3.9**    **Right on Rt. 162.**

**5.9**    **Right to stay on Rt. 162 where Creek Rd. continues straight.**

7.3    Intersect Rt. 3051; Star Gazer Stone Historic Marker.

**8.0**    **Right on Brandywine Dr.**

9.5    Intersect Fourpath Rd.

**10.3**    **Left on Northbrook Rd.**

10.9    Intersect Broad Run Rd.

**11.2**    **Right on Camp Linden Rd.**

**11.8**    **Right on N. Wawaset Rd.**

**12.6**    **Left on Rt. 842.**

**13.5**    **Right on Brandywine Ck. Rd. where Rt. 842 turns left.**

**14.6**    **Right on Rt. 52.**

14.8    Brandywine Picnic Park; continue straight onto Rt. 100.

**16.0**    **Left on Rt. 926.**

**16.2**    **Bear right onto Rt. 100.**

**18.8**    **Right on Hwy. 1.**

18.9    Brandywine Museum.

**19.1**    **Left on Fairville Rd.;** becomes Hillendale Rd.

22.7    Intersect Rt. 52.

**23.5**    **Right on Greenwood Rd.**

**24.6**    **Right on Hwy. 1;** follow signs to Longwood Gardens to loop around and over the highway.

**24.9**    **Bear left at entrance to Gardens onto Longwood Rd.**

25.3    End at the picnic area.

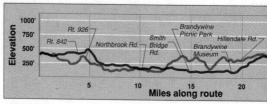

# Delaware

## 22.7 miles

0    Start at the parking lot and picnic area on Longwood Rd. just west of the entrance to Longwood Gardens, head west on Longwood Rd.

**0.2**    **Right on Conservatory Rd.**

0.8    Intersect Rt. 926; **cross over and bear left onto Doe Run Rd.; then immediate right on Folly Hill Rd.**

**2.0**    **Right on Unionville - Lenape Rd.**

**3.5**    **Right on Rt. 52.**

**3.7**    **Left on Parkersville Rd.**

4.6    Intersect Rt. 926.

**5.1**    **Left on Pocopson Rd.**

5.9    Intersect Chandler Rd.

**6.9**    **Right on Rt. 926.**

**7.2**    **Right on Rt. 100 S.**

**9.8**    **Left on Hwy. 1; then immediate right on Rt. 100 S.**

12.1    Intersect Cossart Rd.

13.0    Intersect Twaddle Mill Rd.

**14.0**    **Right on Smith Bridge Rd.** (unmarked - 1st intersection after Twaddle Mill Rd.).

**14.5**    **Left on Pyles Ford Rd.**

15.4    Intersect Rt. 52.

**15.6**    **Right on Old Kennett Rd.** (unmarked).

16.1    Intersect Owls Nest Rd.

17.9    Intersect Center Mill Rd.

**18.9**    **Right on Bayard Rd.**

**19.7**    **Right on Hillendale Rd.**

20.5    Intersect Rosedale Rd.

**20.9**    **Left on Greenwood Rd.**

**22.0**    **Right on Hwy. 1;** follow signs to Longwood Gardens to loop around and over the highway.

**22.3**    **Bear left at entrance to Gardens onto Longwood Rd.**

22.7    End at the picnic area.

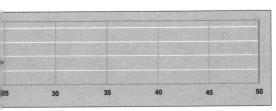

*(continued from page 97)*

meet in Pocopson township. Trees shade much of this part of each route, and a good deal of the roads throughout the area. This is a farmed, rolling landscape in transition to being more suburbanized and developed. Traffic gravitates quickly to the main thoroughfares, leaving the many narrow country roads relatively quiet and well-suited for bicycle exploration.

## Notes:

_____

_____

_____

_____

_____

_____

_____

# Calorie Counter

**Wawaset: 25.3 miles**

| Average Speed (mph) | Riding Time | Calories Expended* |
|---|---|---|
| 5 | 5 hrs. 2 mins. | 690 |
| 10 | 2 hrs. 31 mins. | 760 |
| 15 | 1 hr. 41 mins. | 910 |
| 20 | 1 hr. 16 mins. | 1320 |

**Delaware: 22.7 miles**

| Average Speed (mph) | Riding Time | Calories Expended* |
|---|---|---|
| 5 | 4 hrs. 32 mins. | 630 |
| 10 | 2 hrs. 16 mins. | 680 |
| 15 | 1 hr. 31 mins. | 810 |
| 20 | 1 hr. 8 mins. | 1180 |

* Estimations from tractive-resistance calculations,
Whitt and Wilson, "Bicycling Science"

# Longwood
## Hill and Dale
### and
## Doe Run

These two loops start at Longwood Gardens just off Hwy. 1. It is an area that is beginning to reflect its proximity to Wilmington and Philadelphia in its land use patterns. You will find more woodlots, large residential lots, and housing developments than on the rides further west - but there are still plenty of purely rural backroads to provide hours of relaxed riding. Some of the best of it comes as you ride through some very pleasant small valleys with grass covered and fenced hillsides.

Longwood Gardens includes over 1,000 acres of
*(continued on page 112)*

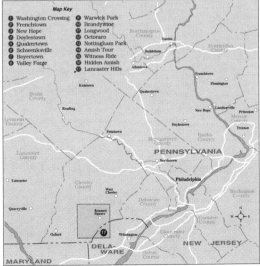

Map Key

1 Washington Crossing
2 Frenchtown
3 New Hope
4 Doylestown
5 Quakertown
6 Schwenksville
7 Boyertown
8 Valley Forge
9 Warwick Park
10 Brandywine
11 Longwood
12 Octoraro
13 Nottingham Park
14 Amish Tour
15 Witness Ride
16 Hidden Amish
17 Lancaster Hills

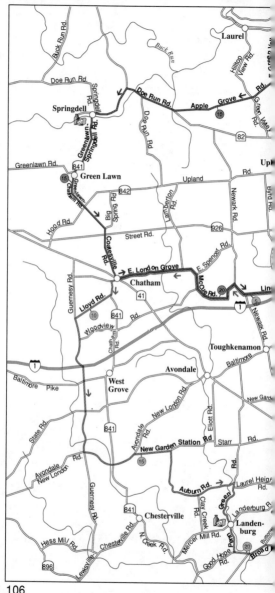

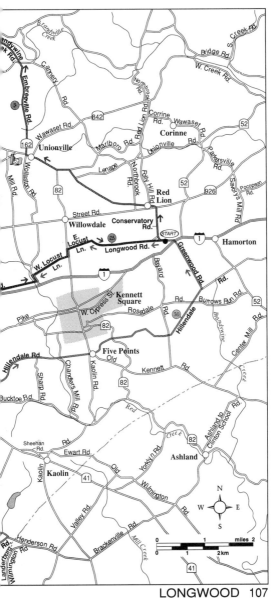

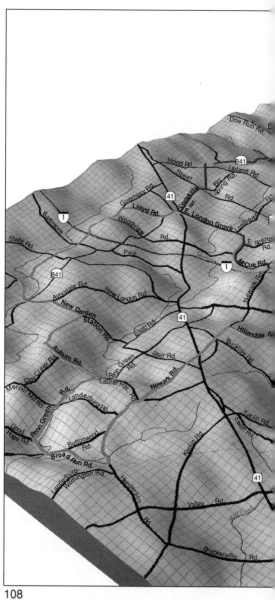

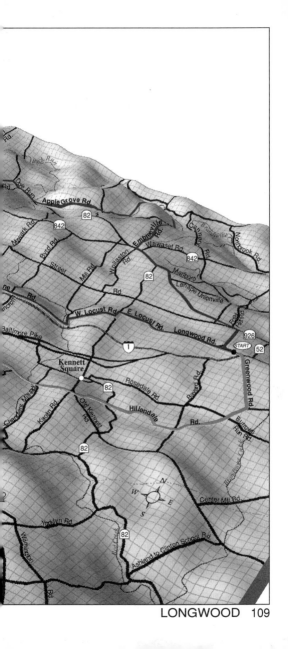

# Hill and Dale

## 32.8 miles

| | |
|---|---|
| 0 | Start at the parking lot and picnic area on Longwood Rd. just west of the entrance to Longwood Gardens; head west on Longwood Rd. |
| 0.2 | Intersect Conservatory Rd. |
| 0.8 | Intersect Schoolhouse Rd. |
| 1.5 | Intersect Walnut Rd.; becomes E. Locust La. |
| **2.2** | **Left on Rt. 82.** |
| **2.3** | **Right on W. Locust La.** |
| **3.3** | **Left on Mill Rd.** |
| **3.4** | **Right on Line Rd.** |
| 4.0 | Intersect Cedar Spring Rd. |
| **5.5** | **Right on Newark Rd.** |
| **5.8** | **Left on London Grove Rd.** (unmarked); becomes Church Rd. |
| **6.2** | **Right on McCue Rd.** |
| **6.9** | **Bear right to stay on McCue Rd. at intersection with Woodview Rd.** |
| **7.3** | **Bear left to stay on McCue Rd.;** becomes London Grove Rd.. |
| 7.7 | Intersect Lamberton Rd. |
| 9.1 | Intersect Rt. 41; cross over and continue straight on London Grove Rd. |
| **9.3** | **Left on Chatam Rd. to stay on Rt. 841.** |
| **9.6** | **Right on Lloyd Rd.** |
| **10.5** | **Left on N. Guernsey Rd.** |
| 11.4 | Intersect Ewing Dr. |
| 11.7 | Cross under Hwy. 1. |
| 12.1 | Intersect W. Evergreen Rd. (Baltimore Pike). |
| 12.7 | Intersect State Rd. |
| **13.6** | **Left on Avondale - New London Rd.** |
| **14.8** | **Bear right onto New Garden Station Rd.** |
| **15.6** | **Right on Auburn Rd.** |
| 16.2 | Intersect Church Hill Rd. |
| 17.1 | Intersect Clay Creek Rd. |
| **18.0** | **Right on Penn Green Rd.** |
| 19.1 | Intersect Mercer Mill Rd. |
| **20.0** | **Left on Good Hope Rd.** (unmarked T-intersection); becomes Broad Run Rd. |
| **21.4** | **Left on Newark Rd.** *(cont. on page 112)* |

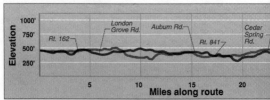

# Doe Run

## 26.6 miles

**0** Start at the parking lot and picnic area on Longwood Rd. just west of the entrance to Longwood Gardens; head west on Longwood Rd.

**0.2** **Right on Conservatory Rd.**

0.8 Intersect Rt. 926; **cross over and bear left onto Doe Run Rd.**

2.6 Intersect Union - Lenape Rd.

**3.2** **Bear right onto Rt. 82.**

3.8 Intersect Rt. 842.

**3.9** **Right on Rt. 162.**

5.9 Continue straight onto Brandywine Creek Rd. where Rt. 162 turns right.

**7.0** **Left at intersection with Harveys Bridge Rd.**

7.3 Continue straight onto Green Valley Rd. (unmarked) where Brandywine Creek Rd. turns right.

8.4 Intersect Powell Rd.

9.0 Intersect Hilltop View Rd.; continue straight onto Apple Grove Rd.

**10.9** **Right on Rt. 82** (unmarked).

**12.1** **Left on Rt. 841.**

13.3 Intersect Hilton Rd.; becomes Greenlawn - Springdell Rd.

14.8 Intersect Sharitz Rd.

15.6 Intersect Rt. 842.

16.5 Intersect Rt. 926.

**17.5** **Left on Rt. 841 (London Grove Rd.).**

18.9 Intersect Lamberton Rd.

**19.3** **Bear right to stay on London Grove Rd.** (unmarked); becomes McCue Rd.

**19.7** **Bear left to stay on McCue Rd. at intersection with Woodview Rd.**

**20.4** **Left on Church Rd.**

**20.8** **Right on Rd. 3033/ Newark Rd.** (unmarked).

**21.1** **Left on Line Rd.**

22.6 Intersect Cedar Spring Rd.

**23.2** **Left on Mill Rd.**

**23.3** **Right on W. Locust La.**

**24.3** **Left on Rt. 82** (unmarked).

**24.4** **Right on E. Locust La.** *(cont. on page 112)*

*(continued from page 105)*

gardens, woodlands, and meadows, with extensive conservatories housing 20 indoor gardens. Also on the grounds is the historic Pierce-du Pont House, several illuminated fountains, and a children's garden and maze. Performing arts events are staged throughout the year. They lie at the heart of a great weekend retreat area where you could combine cycling, sightseeing of local historic sites, entertainment, and a leisurely visit to the gardens.

'Hill and Dale' aptly describes the landscape of this part of Chester County. There are enough hills to provide interest, but they aren't big enough to intimidate.

---

Hill and Dale *(continued from page 110)*
22.0  Intersect Buttonwood Rd.
22.7  Intersect Laurel Heights Rd.
23.4  Intersect Egypt Run Rd.
24.1  Intersect Rt. 41.
**25.1  Right on Hillendale Rd.**
27.0  Intersect Chandler Mill Rd.
27.7  Intersect Koalin Rd.
28.3  Intersect Rt. 82.
30.5  Cross under RR bridge; intersect
      Rosedale Rd.
**31.0  Left on Greenwood Rd.** (Kennett
      Grange #19 on left).
**32.1  Right on Hwy. 1;** follow signs to
      Longwood Gardens to loop around
      and over the highway.
**32.4  Bear left at entrance to Gardens onto
      Longwood Rd.**
32.8  End at the picnic area.

---

Doe Run *(continued from page 111)*
25.1  Intersect Walnut Rd.; becomes
      Longwood Rd.
25.8  Intersect Schoolhouse Rd.
26.4  Intersect Conservatory Rd.
26.6  End at the picnic area.

# Octoraro

## Octoraro Creek
### and
## Chester Farmland

It is hard to go wrong when laying out routes in Chester County – there are always dozens of alternatives just as good as the one picked. These two rides meander through the gently rolling landscape, searching out particularly scenic stretches of highway in an area saturated with country roads in a lovely setting.

This area is less hilly than that found in southern Lancaster County. In addition, the farms are smaller and more broken up with homesites and woods than in the intensely Amish region of mid-Lancaster County. Many miles of paved *(continued on page 120)*

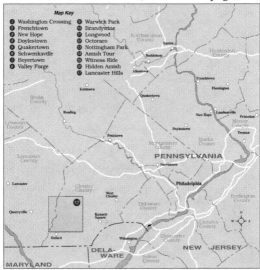

**Map Key**

1. Washington Crossing
2. Frenchtown
3. New Hope
4. Doylestown
5. Quakertown
6. Schwenksville
7. Boyertown
8. Valley Forge
9. Warwick Park
10. Brandywine
11. Longwood
12. Octoraro
13. Nottingham Park
14. Amish Tour
15. Witness Ride
16. Hidden Amish
17. Lancaster Hills

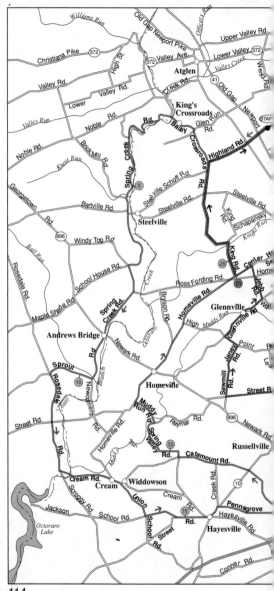

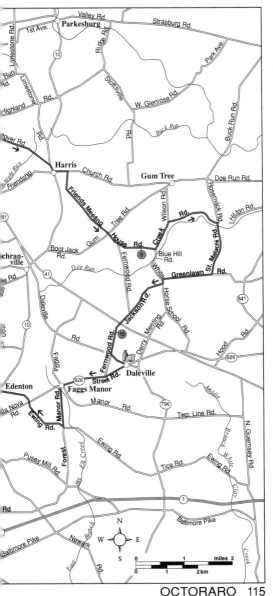

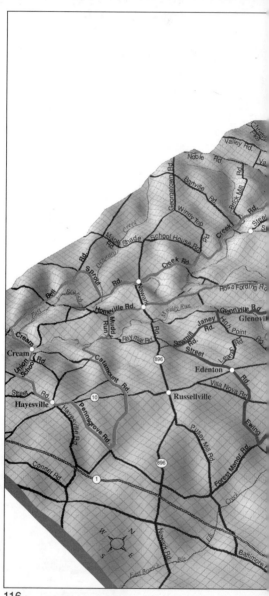

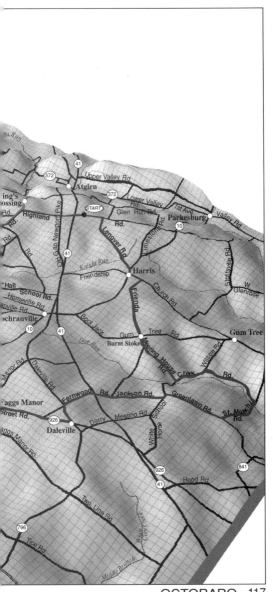

# Octoraro Creek
## 29.5 miles

| | |
|---|---|
| 0 | Start at Octoraro High School just east of Rt. 41 on Highland Rd.; head west on Highland Rd. |
| 0.1 | Intersect Rt. 41. |
| 0.4 | Intersect Old Rt. 41. |
| **1.3** | **Right on Bailey Crossroads Rd.** |
| 2.5 | Covered bridge. |
| **2.6** | **Left on Spring Creek Rd.** |
| 5.2 | Intersect Brick Mill Rd. (unmarked - stucco house on left). |
| 5.4 | Intersect Bartville Rd. |
| **6.8** | **Left to stay on Creek Rd.** (unmarked 4-way intersection). |
| 7.3 | Intersect Ross Fording Rd. |
| 8.3 | Intersect Rt. 896; straight onto Sproul Rd. |
| **10.0** | **Left on Bell Rd.** |
| 11.0 | Intersect Street Rd. |
| **12.0** | **Bear left onto Mt. Eden Rd.** |
| 12.3 | Cross bridge in Chester County; **then left on Cream Rd.** (unmarked). |
| **13.1** | **Right on Union School Rd.** |
| **13.4** | **Keep right at intersection with Widdowson Rd.** (unmarked). |
| **14.3** | **Left on Jackson School Rd.** (unmarked 4-way intersection). |
| **14.9** | **Bear left onto Street Rd.** |
| **15.6** | **Left on Rt. 10.** |
| **15.9** | **Right on Pennsgrove Rd.** |
| **17.0** | **Left on Cullen Rd.** |
| **18.1** | **Right on Rt. 10; then left on Catamount Rd.** |
| **19.6** | **Right on Spring Valley Rd.** |
| **20.5** | **Right on Muddy Run Rd.** |
| **20.8** | **Left at intersection with Ray-Mar to stay on Muddy Run Rd.** |
| **21.4** | **Right on Street Rd.** |
| **21.5** | **Bear left on Homeville Rd.** |
| 22.1 | Intersect Rt. 896. |
| 23.2 | Intersect High Point Rd. |

*(cont. on page 120)*

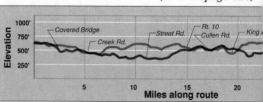

118

# Chester Farmland

## 23.4 miles

Start at Octoraro High School just east of Rt. 41 on Highland Rd.; head east on Highland Rd.

- **.6**   **Right on Lenover Rd.**
- **.2**   **Right on Rt. 10.**
- **.6**   **Left on Friendship Church Rd.**
- **.9**   **Right on Friends Meeting House Rd.**
- .3   Intersect Gum Tree Rd. (unmarked).
- .6   Intersect Fernwood Rd.; **bear left to stay on Friends Meeting House Rd.**
- **.4**   **Left on Creek Rd.**
- **.9**   **Bear right at unmarked Y intersection with Wilson Rd.** (do not go uphill - proceed through open gate).
- **.0**   **Right at St. Malachi Rd.** (unmarked).
- **.9**   **Right on Greenlawn Rd.**
- **.9**   **Left on Whitehorse School Rd.**
- **.0**   **Right on Jackson Rd.**
- .9   Intersect Fernwood Rd.
- 0.2   Intersect Rt. 41.
- **0.8**   **Left on Daleville Rd.** (unmarked 4-way intersection).
- **1.2**   **Right on Rt. 926.**
- 1.7   Intersect Fernwood Rd.
- 1.8   Intersect Baker Rd.
- **2.5**   **Left on Faggs Manor Rd.;** then straight onto Forest Manor Rd.
- **3.3**   **Right on Ewing Rd.**
- 4.3   Intersect Rt. 926; continue straight onto Street Rd.
- 5.0   Intersect Rt. 10.
- **6.3**   **Right on Sawmill Rd.**
- **7.4**   **Left on High Point Rd.** (unmarked T-intersection).
- **7.7**   **Right on Glennville Rd.**
- **8.7**   **Left on Jebb Rd.**
- **9.1**   **Left on Center Hall School Rd.** (unmarked T-intersection).
- **9.5**   **Right on King Rd.**
- **20.3**   **Left on Bailey Crossroads Rd.**

*(cont. on page 120)*

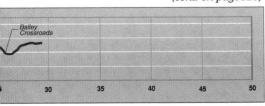

*(continued from page 113)*

backroads, low traffic volume, and a gentle (though not flat) topography combine to make this ideal cycling country.

---

Octoraro Creek *(continued from page 118)*
24.5  Intersect Ross Fording Rd.;  continue
      straight onto Center Hall School Rd.
**24.6  Left on King Rd.**
**25.4  Left on Bailey Crossroads Rd.**
26.7  Intersect Steelville Rd. (unmarked).
**27.3  Bear right on Highland Rd.**
28.1  Intersect Old Rt. 41.
28.4  Intersect Rt. 41.
29.5  End at the high school.

---

Chester Farmland *(continued from page 119)*
21.6  Intersect Steelville Rd. (unmarked).
**22.2  Bear right on Highland Rd.**
23.0  Intersect Old Rt. 41.
23.3  Intersect Rt. 41.
23.4  End at the high school.

---

# Calorie Counter

## Octoraro Creek:  29.5 miles

| Average Speed (mph) | Riding Time | Calories Expended* |
|---|---|---|
| 5 | 5 hrs. 54 mins. | 820 |
| 10 | 2 hrs. 57 mins. | 880 |
| 15 | 1 hr.  57 mins. | 1060 |
| 20 | 1 hr.  28 mins. | 1540 |

## Chester Farmland:  23.4 miles

| Average Speed (mph) | Riding Time | Calories Expended* |
|---|---|---|
| 5 | 4 hrs. 40 mins. | 650 |
| 10 | 2 hrs. 20 mins. | 700 |
| 15 | 1 hr.  33 mins. | 830 |
| 20 | 1 hr.  10 mins. | 1220 |

\* Estimations from tractive-resistance calculations,
Whitt and Wilson, "Bicycling Science"

# Nottingham Park
## Blue Ball
### and
## Oxford

These two rides explore more southern Chester County farmland, with the longer ride dipping down into Maryland. They cover an easy-going, rolling landscape of small housing developments. The town of Oxford is pleasant, and offers a choice of restaurants and food stores.

The starting point for both rides is Nottingham Park, an extensive facility with picnic tables, water, toilets, and parking. While both rides are fairly short, they could be combined or added to for a ride of any length.

*(continued on page 128)*

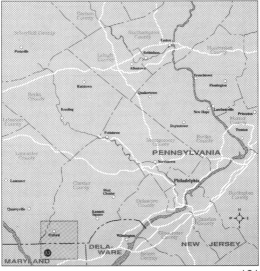

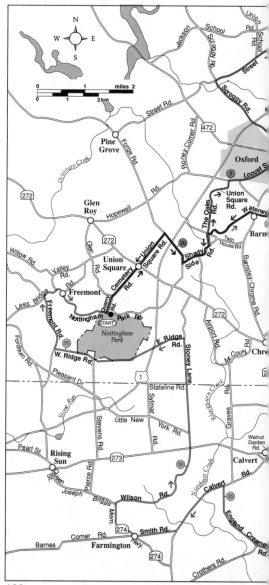

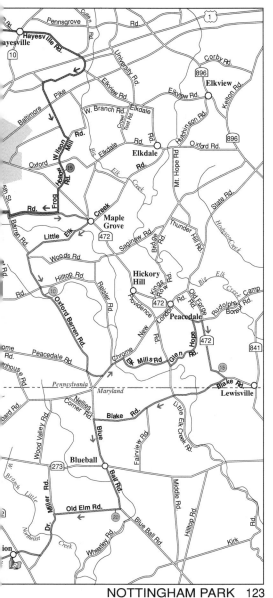

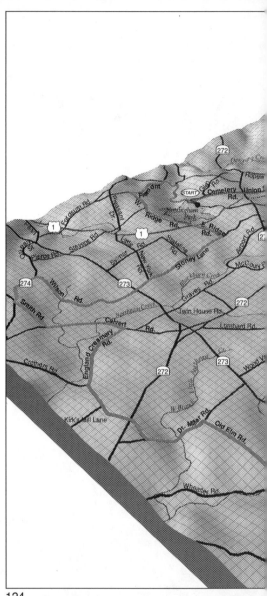

# Blue Ball

## 38.2 miles

| | |
|---|---|
| 0 | Start at the entrance to Nottingham Park; head west on Park Rd. |
| **0.2** | **Right on Cemetery Rd.** |
| **0.5** | **Right at intersection with Glenroy to stay on Cemetery Rd.** |
| 1.3 | Intersect Rt. 272; continue straight on Union Square Rd. |
| **2.1** | **Right on Forge Rd.** |
| 2.3 | Cross over Hwy. 1. |
| **2.8** | **Left on Shadyside Rd.** |
| **3.3** | **Bear left to stay on Shadyside Rd.** |
| **3.4** | **Bear left on The Oaks Rd.** |
| **3.7** | **Right on Twin House Rd.** |
| **3.8** | **Left on Waterway Rd.** |
| 4.8 | Intersect Rt. 131. |
| 5.3 | Intersect Mt. Pleasant Rd. |
| **5.9** | **Right on 5th St.; then left to continue on Waterway Rd.** |
| 6.9 | Intersect Frog Hollow Rd. |
| **7.5** | **Right on Little Elk Creek Rd. just before Rt. 472.** |
| **9.0** | **Left on 5th St./ Oxford Banen Rd.** |
| 9.7 | Intersect Media Rd. |
| **10.6** | **Left on Peacedale Rd.** (unmarked). |
| **11.4** | **Right on Rogers Rd.** |
| 12.5 | Continue straight at unmarked 4-way intersection. |
| 13.2 | Intersect Breckenridge Rd. |
| **13.7** | **Right on Lewisville Rd. (Rt. 472).** |
| **13.9** | **Right to stay on Rt. 472.** |
| **15.2** | **Right on Blake Rd.** |
| 16.2 | Intersect Little Elk Creek Rd. |
| **18.0** | **Left on Blue Ball Rd.** (unmarked T-intersection). |
| 18.9 | Intersect Rt. 273. |
| **19.8** | **Right on Old Elm Rd.** (1st right after Rt. 273). |
| **21.1** | **Left on Dr. Miller Rd.** (unmarked T-intersection). |
| **21.9** | **Right on England Creamery Rd.** |
| 22.5 | Intersect Rt. 272. *(cont. on page 128)* |

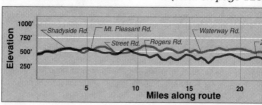

# Oxford

## 22.6 miles

)   Start at the entrance to Nottingham Park; head west on Park Rd.

**0.2  Right on Cemetery Rd.**

**0.5  Right at intersection with Glenroy to stay on Cemetery Rd.**

1.3  Intersect Rt. 272; continue straight on Union Square Rd.

**2.1  Right on Forge Rd.**

2.3  Cross over Hwy. 1.

**2.8  Left on Shadyside Rd.**

**3.3  Bear left to stay on Shadyside Rd.**

**3.4  Bear left on The Oaks Rd.**

3.7  Intersect Twin House Rd.

**4.3  Right on Union Square Rd.**

**5.0  Right on Locust St.**

**6.0  Left on Western Terrace.**

**6.1  Right;** becomes Coach Rd.

6.2  Cross Rt. 472, **then left on Pine St.**

7.0  Cross over Hwy. 1.

**8.2  Right on Street Rd.**

9.1  Intersect Union School Rd.

10.5  Intersect Rt. 10; becomes Hayesville Rd.

11.8  Cross over Hwy. 1.

**12.1  Right on Conner Rd.**

**13.0  Left on Reedville Rd.** (unmarked 4-way intersection).

13.4  Cross over Old Rt. 1.

**14.2  Right on Wilson Mill Rd.**

**14.5  Bear left at intersection with Locust Rd. to stay on Wilson Mill Rd.**

14.7  Intersect Lions Bone Mill Rd.; continue straight onto Frog Hollow Rd.

15.2  Intersect Rt. 472.

15.3  Intersect Falton Rd.

**15.7  Right on Waterway Rd.**

**16.7  Right on 5th St.; then left to continue on Waterway Rd.**

17.3  Intersect Mt. Pleasant Ave.

17.8  Intersect Rt. 131.

**18.8  Right on Twin House Rd.**

**18.9  Left on The Oaks Rd.** *(cont. on page 128)*

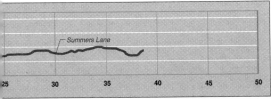

Summers Lane

25    30    35    40    45    50

*(continued from page 121)*

There are many unmarked intersections around here, and taking along a street map is always a good idea. There are enough roads criss-crossing the area to allow you to quickly regain your bearings if you do make a wrong turn.

---

Blue Ball *(continued from page 126)*
22.6 Zion.
23.6 Intersect Trinity Church Rd.
**25.3 Left on Calvert Rd.** (unmarked T- intersection).
**26.6 Right on Smith Rd.**
**27.5 Right on Rt. 274 (Memorial Hwy.).**
**28.3 Right on Wilson Rd.**
30.1 Intersect Summers Lane.
30.5 Intersect Rt. 273.
31.7 Intersect State Line Rd.; becomes Stoney Ln.
**32.6 Left on E. Ridge Rd.**
33.2 Intersect Hwy. 1.
**35.2 Right on Freemont Rd.**
**36.3 Right on Lees Bridge Rd.**
36.7 Continue straight onto Park Rd. where Lees Bridge Rd. turns left.
38.2 End at the entrance to Nottingham Park.

---

Oxford *(continued from page 127)*
**19.2 Bear right on Shadyside Rd.**
**19.8 Right on Forge Rd.**
20.3 Cross over Hwy. 1.
**20.5 Left on Union Square Rd.**
21.3 Intersect Rt. 272; continue straight onto Cemetery Rd.
**22.1 Left at intersection with Glenroy to stay on Cemetery Rd.**
**22.4 Left on Park Rd.**
22.6 End at the entrance to the park.

# Amish Tour
## Covered Bridges
### and
## New Holland

These two rides take you through miles of classic Amish farm country. Large, productive farms with their traditional looking houses and barns line quiet country lanes that seem made for bicycles and buggies. There are seven covered bridges on the long ride, and more to be found if you take along a county map and make a few detours. The floor-boards of these bridges run parallel to the road, so it is safest to walk your bike across them.

Be sure to pack food and water with you on both routes. Although there are many villages marked on the map, most have no services.

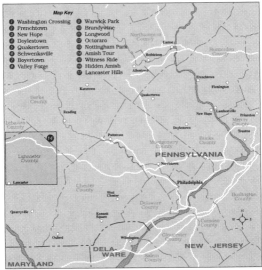

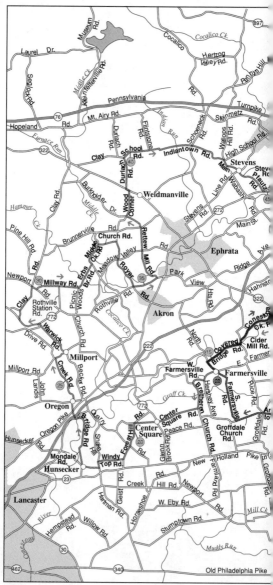

130

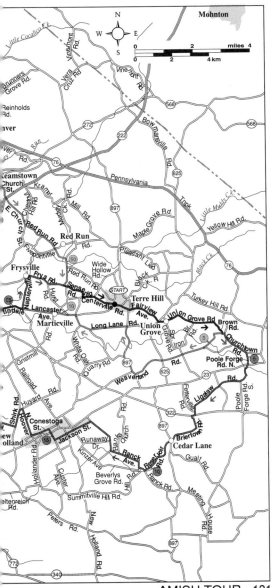

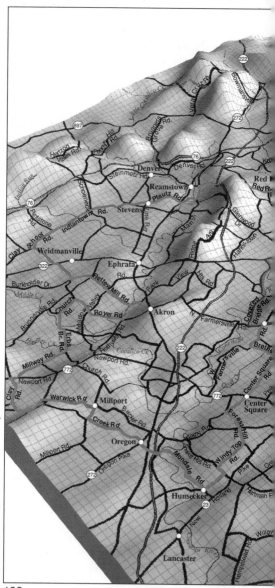

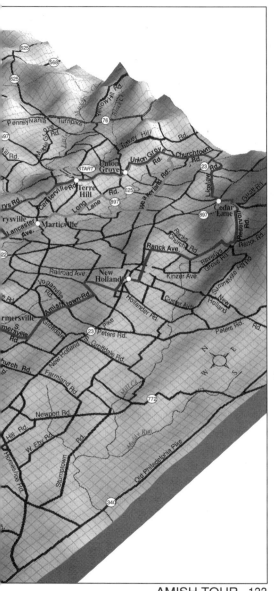

# Covered Bridges

## 52.3 miles

| | |
|---|---|
| 0 | Start in Terre Hill at Main St. and Rt. 897 N.; head east on Main St. |
| 0.7 | Intersect Rt. 897 S. |
| 1.6 | Intersect Rt. 625 (Reading Rd.). |
| 1.9 | Continue straight onto Union Grove Rd. |
| **3.8** | **Right on Weaverland Rd.** |
| 4.4 | Covered bridge. |
| 5.4 | Intersect Spring Grove Rd. |
| 6.0 | Intersect Rt. 625. |
| 6.4 | Intersect Conestoga Creek Rd. |
| **7.2** | **Keep left after one lane bridge.** |
| **7.4** | **Right on Rt. 897.** |
| **7.8** | **Left on Long Lane Rd.** |
| 8.6 | Intersect Quarry Rd. |
| **9.0** | **Right on Martindale Rd.** |
| **9.6** | **Left at unmarked T-intersection (Lancaster Rd.) to stay on Martindale Rd.** |
| 10.0 | Intersect Hurst Rd. |
| 10.2 | Intersect Gristmill Rd.;  Marticville. |
| **12.3** | **Right on Rt. 322.** |
| **12.7** | **Left on Cabin Rd.** |
| **14.2** | **Left on Cider Mill Rd.** |
| **14.3** | **Right on Covered Bridge Rd. after covered bridge.** |
| **15.6** | **Left on Farmersville Rd.** |
| **16.0** | **Right on W. Farmersville Rd.** |
| **16.8** | **Left on Brethren Church Rd.** |
| **17.7** | **Right on Center Square Rd.** |
| 19.0 | Intersect Rt. 722. |
| **19.7** | **Left on Forest Hill Rd.** |
| **20.8** | **Right on Windy Top Rd.** |
| **21.6** | **Left on Snake Hill Rd.** |
| **21.8** | **Right on Hunsecker Rd.** |
| **22.3** | **Right on Mondale Rd.** |
| **23.4** | **Left on Bridge Rd.** |
| 24.0 | Covered bridge. |
| **24.1** | **Right on Creek Rd.** |
| **24.6** | **Right on Rt. 722;   then left on Creek Rd.** |
| **26.2** | **Right on Millport Rd.** |
| **26.4** | **Left on Warwick Rd.** |

*(cont. on page 136)*

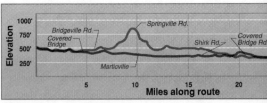

# New Holland

## 29.9 miles

| | |
|---|---|
| 0 | Start in Terre Hill at Main St. and Rt. 897 N.; head east on Main St. |
| 0.7 | Intersect Rt. 897 S. |
| 1.6 | Intersect Rt. 625 (Reading Rd.). |
| 1.9 | Continue straight onto Union Grove Rd. |
| 3.8 | Intersect Weaverland Rd.; continue straight onto Churchtown Rd. |
| **4.8** | **Right on Poole Forge Rd. N.** |
| **5.2** | **Right on Rt. 23; then left on Poole Forge Rd. after bridge.** |
| **5.6** | **Bear right to stay on Poole Forge Rd. at intersection with Nolt Rd.** |
| **5.9** | **Right on Ligalaw Rd.** |
| 6.7 | Intersect Bridgeville Rd. |
| 7.8 | Intersect Fetterville Rd. |
| **7.9** | **Right on Rt. 322.** |
| **8.0** | **Left on Briertown Rd.** |
| **9.6** | **Right on Springville Rd. (Rt. 897); then left on Reservoir Rd.** |
| **10.9** | **Right on Ranck Ave.** |
| **11.1** | **Right at intersection with Wallace Rd. to stay on Ranck Rd.** |
| **12.3** | **Right at intersection with Trailer Rd. to stay on Ranck Rd.** |
| **13.4** | **Left on Jackson St.** |
| 14.0 | Intersect Kinser Ave. |
| **14.7** | **Right on Custer Ave.** |
| 14.9 | Intersect Rt. 23. |
| **15.2** | **Left on Conestoga St.** |
| **15.7** | **Right on Hoover Ave.** |
| **16.5** | **Left on Huyard Rd.** |
| **16.6** | **Left on Shirk Rd.** |
| **17.1** | **Right on Amishtown Rd.** |
| **17.9** | **Right on Voganville Rd.** |
| **18.0** | **Left on Amishtown Rd.** |
| 18.6 | Straight at 5-way intersection onto Groffdale Church Rd. |
| **19.4** | **Right on S. Farmersville Rd.** |
| **21.5** | **Right on Covered Bridge Rd.** |
| **22.7** | **Left to cross covered bridge.** |

*(cont. on page 136)*

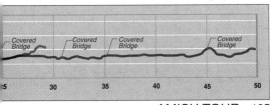

**27.8 Left on Rothville Rd. (Rt. 772).**
**28.6 Right on Clay Rd.**
**29.6 Right on Newport Rd.**
**29.7 Left on Millway Rd.**
**31.1 Left on Erbs Bridge Rd. at intersection with Picnic Woods Rd.**
31.5 Covered bridge.
**32.0 Left on Middle Creek Rd.**
**32.6 Right on Church Rd.**
**33.2 Right on Royer Rd.**
33.7 Intersect Meadow Valley Rd.
**34.8 Left on Rothville Rd.**
**35.6 Left on Rettew Mill Rd.**
35.8 Covered bridge.
36.8 Intersect Meadow Valley Rd.
**38.0 Right on Wood Corner Rd.**
**38.8 Left on Rt. 322 then right on Durlach Rd.**
**39.9 Right on Clay School Rd. (unmarked T-intersection);** becomes Indiantown Rd.
42.2 Intersect Schoeneck Rd.
**43.4 Left on Main St.**
43.8 Intersect Line Rd.; continue straight onto Stevens Rd.
**44.3 Right on Pfautz Rd.**
44.8 Intersect Rt. 272.
**45.2 Right on Creek Rd. (unmarked T-intersection);** covered bridge.
**45.6 Left on Reamstown Rd.**
**46.1 Right on Church St.**
46.8 Cross under Rt. 222.
**47.8 Left on Red Run Rd.**
49.7 Intersect Martin Church Rd.; covered bridge.
49.9 Continue straight onto Gristmill Rd. where Red Run Rd. turns left.
**50.5 Left on Sensenig Rd.**
**51.2 Left on Centerville Rd.**
**51.6 Right to stay on Centerville Rd.**
52.3 End in Terre Hill at Rt. 897 N.

---

**22.9 Right on Conestoga Creek Rd.**
**24.4 Right on Rt. 322.**
**24.7 Left on Martindale Rd.**
**25.9 Left on Napierville Rd.**
**26.9 Right on Frys Rd.**
**27.7 Left on Sensenig Rd.**
28.1 Intersect Gristmill Rd.
**28.8 Left on Centerville Rd.**
**29.1 Right to stay on Centerville Rd.**
29.9 End in Terre Hill at Rt. 897 N.

# Witness
## Strasburg
### and
## Amish Farms

The Witness rides are named for the movie, which was filmed at a farm along the Strasburg route. This is the heart of Amish farm country, and a beautiful area for cycling. The countryside is laced with paved roads that offer an infinite variety in routes. The two rides detailed here wind through some of the prettiest landscape in the region, and include many short sections of particularly scenic roadways. Once you have negotiated one or both of these routes, it will be easy to design your own for many days of exploring.

*(continued on page 144)*

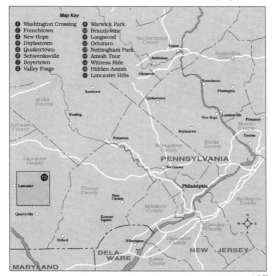

**Map Key**
1. Washington Crossing
2. Frenchtown
3. New Hope
4. Doylestown
5. Quakertown
6. Schwenksville
7. Boyertown
8. Valley Forge
9. Warwick Park
10. Brandywine
11. Longwood
12. Octoraro
13. Nottingham Park
14. Amish Tour
15. Witness Ride
16. Hidden Amish
17. Lancaster Hills

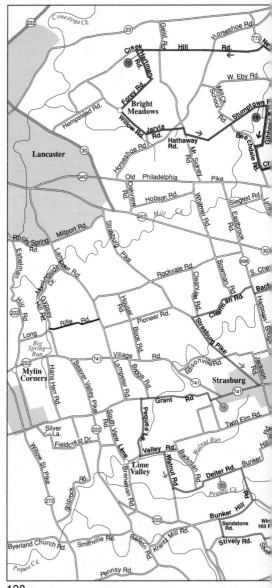

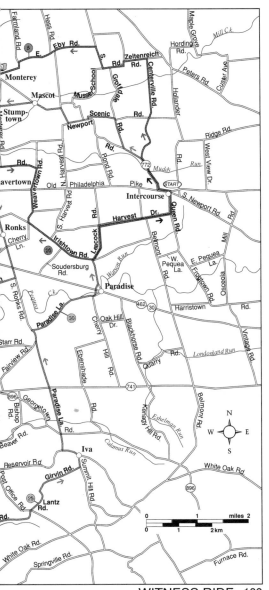

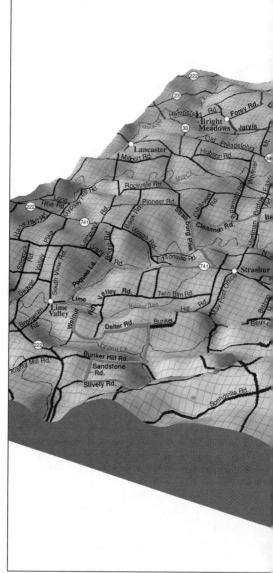

# Strasburg
## 33.8 miles

| | |
|---|---|
| 0 | Start in Intercourse at the entrance to Kitchen Kettle Village; head west on Rt. 340. |
| **0.1** | **Right on W. Newport Rd. (Rt. 772).** |
| 0.7 | Intersect Centerville Rd. |
| **1.2** | **Right on Groffdale Rd.** |
| **1.8** | **Left on Scenic Rd.** |
| **2.4** | **Right on Newport Rd. (Rt. 772).** |
| **2.9** | **Right to stay on Newport Rd. where Harvest Rd. goes straight.** |
| **3.2** | **Left to stay on Newport Rd. where Harvest Rd. goes straight.** |
| **3.8** | **Left on Stumptown Rd.** |
| 4.5 | Intersect Monterey Rd. |
| **5.1** | **Left on Gibbons Rd.** |
| 5.6 | Bird in Hand Bake Shop. |
| **6.1** | **Left on Beechdale Rd.** |
| **6.6** | **Left on Church Rd.** |
| **7.0** | **Right on Ronks Rd.** |
| 7.5 | Intersect Rt. 340. |
| 9.0 | Intersect Rt. 30. |
| **9.2** | **Right on Bachmantown Rd.** (unmarked - at signal). |
| **10.7** | **Right on Rt. 896.** |
| **10.8** | **Left on Leaman Rd.** |
| **12.2** | **Left on Strasburg Pike.** |
| **14.1** | **Right on Rt. 741.** |
| 14.9 | Continue straight onto Lime Valley Rd. where Rt. 741 bears right. |
| **15.1** | **Right on Hagers Rd.;** becomes Penn Grant Rd. |
| 16.4 | Covered bridge. |
| **16.6** | **Left on Pequea Lane.** |
| **17.7** | **Left on Lime Valley Rd.** |
| **18.2** | **Right on Walnut Run Rd.** |
| **19.0** | **Left on Deiter Rd.** |
| 19.5 | Intersect Backman Rd. |
| **20.5** | **Right on Bunker Hill Rd.** |
| **21.2** | **Right at intersection with Weaver Rd. to stay on Bunker Hill Rd.** |
| **22.0** | **Left on Sandstone Rd.** |
| **22.3** | **Left on Stively Rd.** *(cont. on page 144)* |

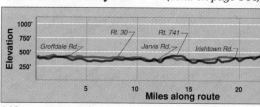

# Amish Farms

## 23.5 miles

Start in Intercourse at the entrance to Kitchen Kettle Village; head west on Rt. 340.

- **.1 Right on W. Newport Rd. (Rt. 772).**
- .7 Straight on Centerville Rd. where Rt. 772 bears left.
- .6 Intersect Scenic Rd.
- **.8 Left on Zeltenreich Rd.**
- **.2 Left on Musser School Rd.**
- **.7 Right on Groffdale Rd.**
- **.2 Left on Eby Rd.** (unmarked - first left).
- .5 Intersect Stumptown Rd.
- **.8 Left on Farmland Rd.**
- **.3 Right on Newport Rd. (Rt. 772).**
- **.3 Left on Creek Hill Rd.**
- .3 Intersect Horseshoe Rd.
- .4 Intersect Geist Rd.
- **.9 Left on Hartman Rd.** (unmarked - just before marked Hartman Rd. turns right).
- **0.6 Right on Forey Rd.**
- **1.6 Left on Willow Rd.** (unmarked T-intersection).
- **2.3 Left on Jarvis Rd.**
- **2.8 Left on Horseshoe Rd.; then right on Hathaway Rd.**
- **3.1 Right on Mt. Sidney Rd.** (unmarked T-intersection).
- **3.4 Left on Stumptown Rd.** (unmarked road between two brick houses).
- **5.1 Right on Gibbons Rd.**
- 5.5 Bird in Hand Bake Shop.
- **.6.0 Left on Beechdale Rd.**
- **.6.5 Left on Church Rd.**
- 7.0 Intersect Ronks Rd.
- **.8.1 Right on N. Weavertown Rd.**
- .8.6 Intersect Rt. 340.
- **.9.3 Left on Irishtown Rd.**
- **0.8 Left on Leacock Rd.**
- **1.5 Right on Harvest Rd.**
- **2.9 Left on Queen Rd.**
- **3.3 Left on Newport Rd. (Rt. 772).**
- **3.4 Left on Rt. 340;** end in Intercourse.

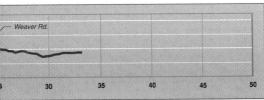

*(continued from page 137)*

Food is generally available only in the larger towns throughout this area. Both routes do, however, pass by a favorite bakery of local cyclists. Strasburg is a pleasant town with several Bed and Breakfast Inns and a few restaurants and food stores.

---

Strasburg *(continued from page 142)*
**23.2 Left on Winter Hill Rd.**
23.8 Intersect Weaver Rd.
24.8 Intersect Office Rd., becomes Lantz Rd.
**25.2 Left on Strubel Rd.**
**26.4 Left on Summit Hill Rd.** (unmarked T-intersection).
**26.6 Left on Iva Rd.**
**26.9 Right on Paradise Lane.**
27.2 Intersect Rt. 896, jog right.
28.1 Intersect Rt. 741.
28.4 Toy Train Museum.
**29.3 Right to stay on Paradise Lane where Ronks Rd. bears left.**
30.9 Cross over Rt. 30.
**31.1 Left on Leacock Rd.**
**31.8 Right on Harvest Dr.**
**33.2 Left on Queen Rd.**
**33.6 Left on Newport Rd. (Rt. 772).**
**33.7 Left on Rt. 340.**
33.8 End in Intercourse.

## Calorie Counter

### Strasburg: 33.8 miles

| Average Speed (mph) | Riding Time | Calories Expended* |
|---|---|---|
| 5 | 6 hrs. 58 mins. | 990 |
| 10 | 3 hrs. 28 mins. | 1090 |
| 15 | 2 hrs. 19 mins. | 1390 |
| 20 | 1 hr. 44 mins. | 1900 |

### Amish Farms: 23.5 miles

| Average Speed (mph) | Riding Time | Calories Expended* |
|---|---|---|
| 5 | 4 hrs. 42 mins. | 650 |
| 10 | 2 hrs. 21 mins. | 700 |
| 15 | 1 hr. 33 mins. | 830 |
| 20 | 1 hr. 10 mins. | 1220 |

* Estimations from tractive-resistance calculations, Whitt and Wilson, "Bicycling Science"

# Hidden Amish
## Susquehanna Overlook
### and
## Conowingo Creek

This is an area into which the Amish have expanded as families look for affordable and farmable land in Lancaster County. The Amish influence is not as evident as it is further north, but the occassional horse and buggy, and country roads scarred by tell-tale wagon wheel marks, are pleasant reminders of their presence.

This part of the county is hillier and more forested than to the north. One of the nicest stretches of road in the region is used by both routes – along Oregon Hollow and Scalpy Hollow Rds. It runs several miles along a stream and under a cool,

*(continued on page 152)*

**Map Key**

1. Washington Crossing
2. Frenchtown
3. New Hope
4. Doylestown
5. Quakertown
6. Schwenksville
7. Boyertown
8. Valley Forge
9. Warwick Park
10. Brandywine
11. Longwood
12. Octoraro
13. Nottingham Park
14. Amish Tour
15. Witness Ride
16. Hidden Amish
17. Lancaster Hills

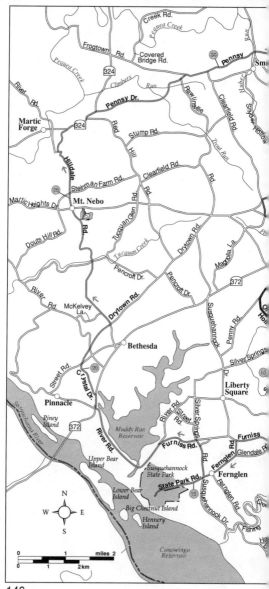

146

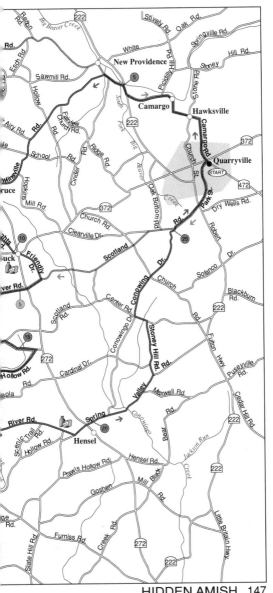

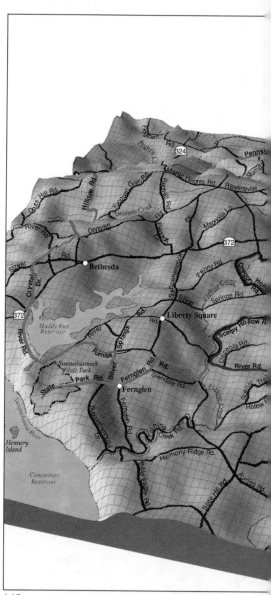

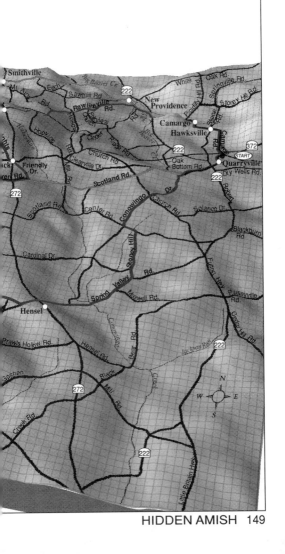

# Susquehanna Overlook

## 37 miles

| | |
|---|---|
| 0 | Start in Quarryville at the elementary school between 3rd and 4th Sts. on Hess St.; head south on Hess St. |
| **0.2** | **Right on Park St.** |
| **0.8** | **Left on Rt. 222; then right on Scotland R**( |
| 2.0 | Intersect Clearview Rd.; **bear left to stay on Scotland Rd.,** |
| 2.4 | Intersect Church Rd. |
| **3.3** | **Bear right onto Deaver Rd.** |
| 3.9 | Intersect Hopkins Mill Rd. |
| 4.4 | Intersect Four Pines Rd. |
| **4.9** | **Jog left; cross Rt. 272.** |
| **6.2** | **Left on Penny Rd.** |
| **6.7** | **Left on Oregon Hollow Rd.** |
| **7.9** | **Left on Silver Springs Rd.** |
| **8.0** | **Right on Oregon Hollow Rd.** |
| **8.6** | **Right on Scalpy Hollow Rd.** |
| 10.9 | Intersect River Rd. |
| **11.2** | **Right on Furniss Rd.** |
| **12.0** | **Left on Fernglen Rd.** |
| **12.2** | **Bear right to stay on Fern Glen Rd. at intersection with Glendale Rd.** |
| 12.8 | Continue straight onto State Park Rd. |
| 13.0 | Intersect Susquehannock Dr.; continue straight into Susquehannock State Park. |
| **14.1** | **Turn around point.** |
| **15.2** | **Left on Susquehannock Dr.** |
| **16.1** | **Left on Furniss Rd.** |
| **17.1** | **Left on River Rd.** |
| **19.1** | **Right on Rt. 372.** |
| **19.3** | **Left on Crystal Dr.** (unmarked - 1st left). |
| **20.1** | **Right on Old Holtwood Rd.** |
| **20.2** | **Left at Drytown Rd.** (unmarked - just after park). |
| 20.5 | Intersect River Rd. |
| **21.1** | **Left on Hilldale Rd.** |
| 22.6 | Intersect Tucquan Glen Rd. |
| 23.8 | Intersect Martic Heights Dr. |
| 24.9 | Intersect Maple Springs Rd. |
| **25.6** | **Right on Marticville Rd. (Rt. 324).** |
| 26.0 | Intersect Red Hill Rd. |

*(cont. on page 152)*

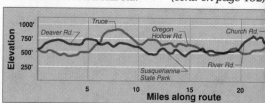

# Conowingo Creek

## 26.4 miles

Start in Quarryville at the elementary school between 3rd and 4th Sts. on Hess St.; head north on Hess St.

| | |
|---|---|
| .2 | **Right on Rt. 372.** |
| .4 | **Left on N. Lime St. where Rt. 472 goes right.** |
| .4 | Intersect Stone Rd.; becomes Camargo Rd. |
| .9 | **Right on Rt. 222.** |
| .0 | **Left on Main St.** |
| .5 | **Left on Truce Rd./Rawlinsville Rd.** |
| .9 | Intersect Hollow Rd. |
| .8 | Intersect Rt. 272 (Lancaster Pike); Truce. |
| .5 | **Left on Clearfield Rd.** |
| .8 | **Left on Buck Heights Rd.** |
| 10.0 | **Left on Rt. 372.** |
| 10.2 | Intersect Rt. 272. |
| 10.3 | **Right on Friendly Dr.** |
| 10.5 | **Left on Four Pines Rd.** |
| 11.1 | **Right on Deaver Rd.** (unmarked T-intersection). |
| 11.6 | **Jog left, cross Rt. 272.** |
| 12.9 | **Left on Penny Rd.** |
| 13.4 | **Left on Oregon Hollow Rd.** |
| 14.6 | **Left on Silver Springs Rd.** |
| 14.7 | **Right on Oregon Hollow Rd.** |
| 15.3 | **Right on Scalpy Hollow Rd.** |
| 17.6 | **Left on River Rd.** |
| | (Note: follow directions on long route to get to State Park.) |
| 19.1 | Intersect Chestnut Level Dr. |
| 19.6 | **Left on Spring Valley Rd.** |
| 19.9 | Intersect Rt. 272 (Lancaster Pike). |
| 20.4 | Intersect Conowingo Rd. |
| 21.6 | **Left on Stony Hill Rd.** |
| 22.7 | **Left on Center Rd.** (unmarked T-intersection). |
| 23.0 | **Right on Conowingo Rd.** |
| 23.8 | Intersect Church Rd. |
| 25.0 | **Bear right on Scotland Rd.** (unmarked T-intersection). |
| 25.6 | **Left on Rt. 222,** *(cont. on page 152)* |

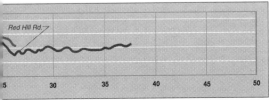

Red Hill Rd.

5    30    35    40    45    50

*(continued from page 145)*

dense canopy of trees. The Susquehanock State Park offers a spectacular view of the Susquehanna River from an overlook high above the river bank.

Be prepared for some real hills, especially on the longer route. Local cyclists use this area for their hill training, and you can count on working up a sweat. Each hill climb takes you to a ridge, however, which often means both a good view of the surrounding countryside and a fun descent into the next valley.

---

Susquehanna Overlook *(continued from page 150)*

26.3 Continue straight onto Pennsy Dr. where
Rt. 324 turns left.
28.3 Intersect Rawlinsville Rd.
29.8 Intersect Rt. 272 (Lancaster Pike).
30.7 Intersect Sawmill Rd.
**31.5 Right at intersection with Refton Rd.**
**33.0 Right on Main St.**
33.2 Intersect Truce Rd.
**33.7 Right on Rt. 222.**
**33.9 Left on Camargo Rd.**
34.6 Intersect Stony Hill Rd.
35.4 Intersect Stone Rd.
36.4 Intersect Rt. 372.
**36.6 Right on Park Ave.**
**36.9 Right on Hess St.**
37.0 End at the elementary school.

---

Conowingo Creek *(continued from page 151)*
**(Robert Fulton Hwy.), then right on S.
Park Ave.**
**26.2 Left on Hess Rd.**
26.4 End at the elementary school.

# Lancaster Hills
## Shady Creek
### and
## Mt. Pleasant

These two rides explore more of hilly southern Lancaster County. Shaded valleys yield to open ridges as you travel through this rolling farm and forest landscape. The trip down Creek Rd. is a well-known delight to local cyclists. It's a cool, tree-covered valley with a small stream and a gentle grade.

While not quite as hilly as the routes directly west of here, there are a couple of good climbs and roaring descents on these loops. And until Brick Mill Rd. is resurfaced, use extra caution coming down this rough road. Riding along the ridges in

*(continued on page 160)*

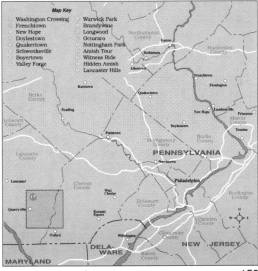

**Map Key**

| | |
|---|---|
| Washington Crossing | Warwick Park |
| Frenchtown | Brandywine |
| New Hope | Longwood |
| Doylestown | Octoraro |
| Quakertown | Nottingham Park |
| Schwenksville | Amish Tour |
| Boyertown | Witness Ride |
| Valley Forge | Hidden Amish |
| | Lancaster Hills |

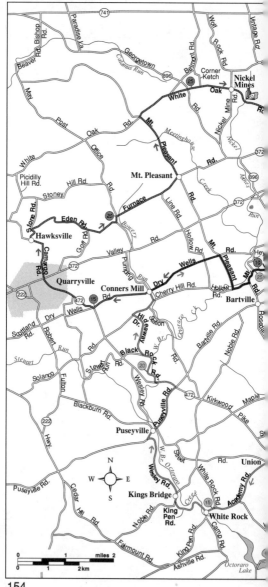

154

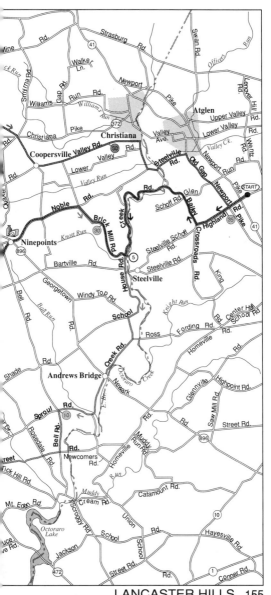

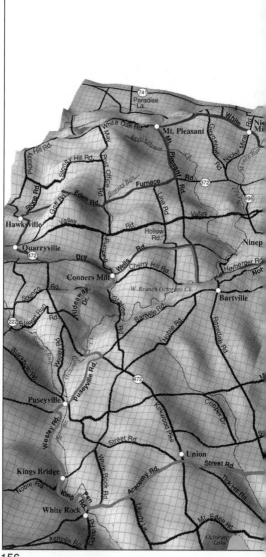

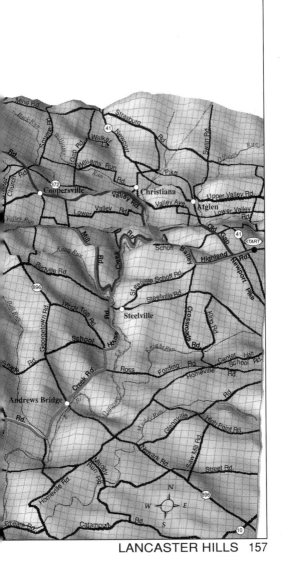

# Shady Creek
## 35.8 miles

| | |
|---|---|
| 0 | Start in Octoraro High School on Highland Rd, just west of Rt. 41; head west on Highland Rd |
| 0.1 | Intersect Rt. 41. |
| 0.4 | Intersect Old Rt. 41. |
| **1.3** | **Right on Bailey Crossroads Rd.** |
| 2.5 | Covered bridge. |
| **2.6** | **Left on Spring Creek Rd.** |
| 5.2 | Intersect Brick Mill Rd. (unmarked – stucco house on left). |
| 5.4 | Intersect Bartville Rd. |
| **6.8** | **Left to stay on Creek Rd.** (unmarked 4-way intersection). |
| 7.3 | Intersect Ross Fording Rd. |
| 8.3 | Intersect Rt. 896; straight onto Sproul Rd. |
| **10.0** | **Left on Bell Rd.** |
| **11.0** | **Right on Street Rd.** |
| 12.8 | Becomes Tick Hill Rd. |
| 13.1 | Intersect Rt. 472. |
| **13.2** | **Left on Academy Rd.** |
| 14.2 | Intersect Liberty Lane (unmarked). |
| **14.3** | **Right to stay on Academy Rd. at** (unmarked **intersection with Liberty Lane.** |
| 15.1 | Straight at intersection with White Rock Rd. (unmarked). |
| 15.2 | Covered bridge; **right on King Pen Rd. (Rt. 490).** |
| **16.1** | **Right on Noble Rd.** |
| **16.2** | **Left on Wesley Rd.** |
| **17.7** | **Right on Puseyville Rd.** (unmarked T-intersection). |
| **19.0** | **Left on Rt. 472 (Kirkwood Pike).** |
| **19.5** | **Right on Black Rock Rd.** |
| **20.4** | **Right on Hideaway Dr.** |
| **21.5** | **Right on Solanco Rd.** (unmarked T-intersection). |
| **21.9** | **Left at next intersection.** |
| **22.3** | **Right at Dry Wells Rd.** |
| 23.7 | Intersect Hollow Rd. |
| **24.1** | **Right on Mt. Pleasant Rd.** |
| 24.9 | Cross covered bridge; **then left to stay on Mt. Pleasant Rd.** *(cont. on page 160)* |

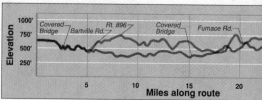

# Mt. Pleasant

## 34.8 miles

| | |
|---|---|
| 0 | Start at Octoraro High School on Highland Rd. just west of Rt. 41;  head west on Highland Rd. |
| 0.1 | Intersect Rt. 41. |
| 0.4 | Intersect Old Rt. 41. |
| **1.3** | **Right on Bailey Crossroads Rd.** |
| 2.5 | Covered bridge. |
| **2.6** | **Left on Spring Creek Rd.** |
| **5.2** | **Right on Brick Mill Rd.** (unmarked – stucco house on left). |
| **6.9** | **Left on Noble Rd.** |
| 7.7 | Intersect White Oak Rd. |
| 8.6 | Intersect Rt. 896 (Georgetown Rd.) |
| **9.3** | **Bear right on Mt. Wilson Rd.** |
| **10.5** | **Right on Mt. Pleasant Rd.** |
| **11.0** | **Right to stay on Mt. Pleasant Rd. at intersection with Hollow Rd.;**  cross covered bridge. |
| **11.8** | **Left on Dry Wells Rd.** |
| 12.2 | Intersect Hollow Rd. |
| 13.6 | Intersect Pumping Station Rd. |
| **14.5** | **Left to stay on Dry Wells Rd.** (unmarked). |
| **15.1** | **Right on Rt. 472** (unmarked). |
| 16.2 | Intersect Park Ave. |
| 16.4 | Intersect Rt. 372;  continue straight onto Camargo Rd. |
| **17.4** | **Right on Stone Rd.** |
| **17.8** | **Right on Eden Rd.** |
| 19.3 | Intersect Groff Rd. |
| **20.1** | **Left on Post Office Rd.** (unmarked T-intersection). |
| **20.2** | **Right on Furnace Rd.** |
| 21.3 | Intersect Hollow Rd. |
| **21.8** | **Left on Mt. Pleasant Rd.** |
| **23.4** | **Right on White Oak Rd.** |
| 24.7 | Intersect Rt. 896 (Georgetown Rd.). |
| 25.8 | Intersect Nickel Mine Rd. |
| 27.0 | Intersect Vintage Rd. |
| 28.0 | Intersect Christiana Pike (Rt. 372). |
| **28.8** | **Left on Valley Rd.** |
| 30.5 | Straight where road splits at intersection with Orchard Buck Rd. *(cont. on page 160)* |

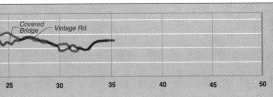

*(continued from page 153)*

this area opens up some great long views over surrounding farmlands and a gentle looking landscape.

---

Shady Creek *(continued from page 158)*
**25.4 Left on Mt. Wilson Rd.**
**26.6 Bear left onto Noble Rd.**
27.3 Intersect Rt. 896 (Georgetown Rd.).
28.2 Intersect White Oak Rd.
**29.0 Right on Brick Mill Rd.**
**30.7 Left on Creek Rd.** (unmarked – at stucco
house); cross wood bridge.
**33.3 Right to cross covered bridge** (unmarked).
**33.4 Right on Bailey Crossroads Rd.** (unmarked).
**34.5 Left on Highland Rd.**
35.4 Intersect Old Rt. 41.
35.7 Intersect Rt. 41.
35.8 End at the high school.

---

Mt. Pleasant *(continued from page 159)*
**31.1 Right at T-intersection; cross under RR
bridge.**
31.3 Intersect Lower Valley Rd.
**31.8 Left on Creek Rd. at intersection with
Noble Rd.**
**32.0 Left to cross bridge** (unmarked); **then
keep left.**
**32.8 Right on Newport Pike (Old Rt. 41)**
(unmarked T-intersection).
33.7 Intersect Glen Run Rd.
**34.4 Left on Highland Rd.**
34.7 Intersect Rt. 41.
34.8 End at the high school.

# Around Southeastern Pennsylvania

Much has been written about this part of the northeast – from both an historic and a tourist perspective. One of the contributors to the rides in this guide, William Hoffman, publishes *Going Dutch*, a comprehensive guidebook to the entire Pennsylvania Dutch Country of southeastern Pennsylvania. Having a companion guide like this can help you plan some interesting side trips or to combine your cycling with other activities in an extended visit to an area. You can contact Bill at Spring Garden Publications Co., Box 7131 J, Lancaster, PA 17604 (717) 560-3636.

## Weather

Southeastern Pennsylvania shares the humid climate of most of the northeastern U.S. For cyclists this means that the combination of heat and humidity on a warm summer day can be taxing and that careful attention be paid to adequate fluid intake. Average summer daytime temperatures for the region are in the low-to mid-80's. It generally cools off into the 60's at night. Summertime rainfall is usually the result of afternoon and evening thunderstorms, and winds are generally westerly and south westerly. Some of the best cycling weather occurs in May and June and in September and October.

## Amish

The lifestyle of the Older Order Amish, many of whom live in the area east of the city of Lancaster, is particularly compatible with bicycle touring. Co-existing with horse-drawn carriage and wagons on small country lanes is easily accomplished. Speed of travel, exposure to the elements, and an increased awareness of the environment are shared by the cyclist and those Amish farmers who shun modern conveniences.

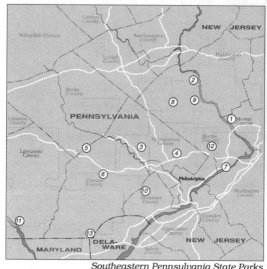

*Southeastern Pennsylvania State Parks*

## State Parks

The map and table on these two pages describe the location and facilities of State Parks in the region covered by this guide. These parks almost always make good rest and picnic stops, and often offer other activities to complement a days ride. Maps and pamphlets for individual parks can be obtained by writing to the bureau of State Parks, Box 1467, Harrisburg, PA 17105-1467. A toll-free information line is also available at 1-800-63 PARKS.

## Valley Forge National Historic Park

The map of Valley Forge National Park on pages 164 and 165 is designed to complement the Valley Forge maps on pages 82 – 85. The paved off-road bike paths, park facilities, and frequent points of interest make this a great area for family bike rides.

## Pennsylvania State Parks

| State Park | Picnicking | Fishing | Swimming | Boating | Camping | Bicycling |
|---|---|---|---|---|---|---|
| ① Washington's Crossing (NJ) | • | • | | • | | |
| ② Delaware Canal | • | • | | • | | • |
| ③ Evansburg | • | • | | | | |
| ④ Fort Washington | • | • | | | | |
| ⑤ French Creek | • | • | • | • | • | |
| ⑥ Marsh Creek | • | • | • | • | | |
| ⑦ Neshaminy | • | • | • | • | | |
| ⑧ Nockamixon | • | • | • | • | | • |
| ⑨ Ralph Stover | • | • | | • | | |
| ⑩ Ridley Creek | • | • | | | | • |
| ⑪ Susquehannock | • | | | | | |
| ⑫ Tyler | • | • | | | • | • |
| ⑬ White Clay Creek | | • | | | | |

## Botanical Gardens

Besides the gardens listed here, there are several wonderful gardens in and near Philadelphia. Long-wood Gardens, located near Kennett Square in Chester County is the starting point for four of our rides, and well worth a visit.

- Bowman's Hill State Wild Flower Preserve (Washington Crossing).
- Brandywine River Museum Wildflower Garden (Chadds Ford).
- Delaware Valley College Gardens (Doylestown).
- Longwood Gardens (Kennett Square).

(continued on page 166)

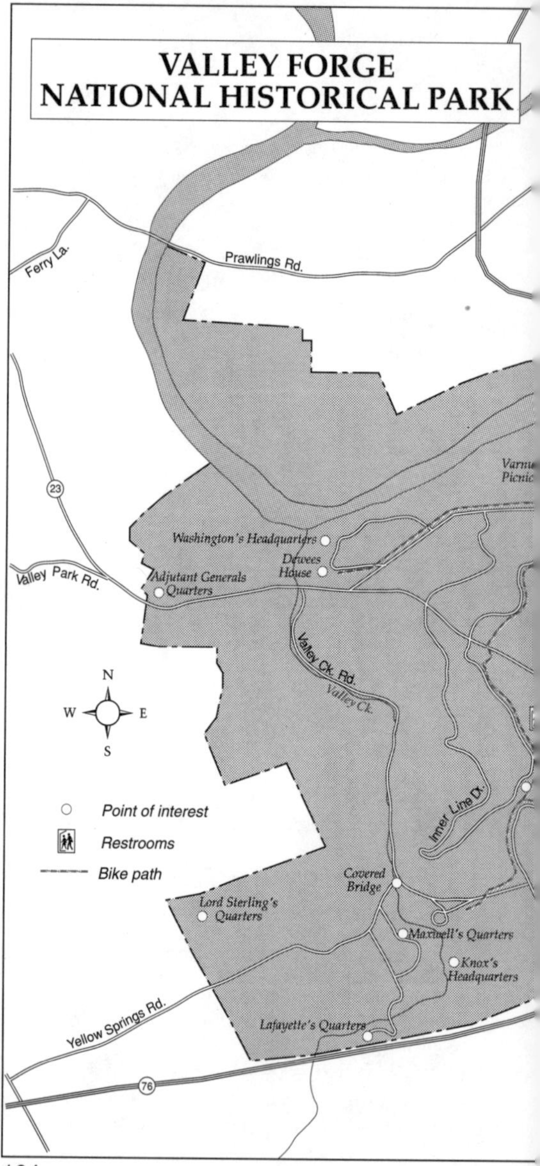

# VALLEY FORGE
# NATIONAL HISTORICAL PARK

Ferry La.

Prawlings Rd.

(23)

Valley Park Rd.

Washington's Headquarters

Dewees House

Adjutant Generals Quarters

Valley Ck. Rd.

Valley Ck.

Varnum
Picnic

Inner Line Dr.

N
W E
S

○     Point of interest

🚹     Restrooms

– – –     Bike path

Lord Sterling's Quarters

Covered Bridge

Maxwell's Quarters

Knox's Headquarters

Yellow Springs Rd.

Lafayette's Quarters

(76)

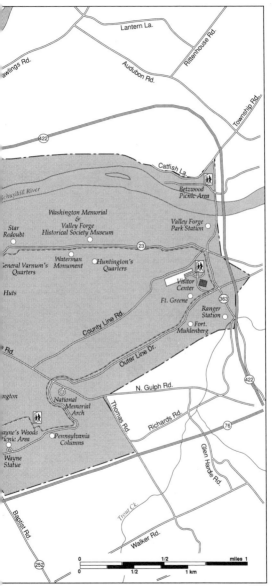

Lantern La.

Rawlings Rd.

Audubon Rd.

Rittenhouse Rd.

Township Rd.

422

Catfish La.

Betzwood
Picnic Area

Schuylkill River

Washington Memorial
&
Valley Forge
Historical Society Museum

Valley Forge
Park Station

Star
Redoubt

23

Waterman
Monument

Huntington's
Quarters

General Varnum's
Quarters

Huts

Visitor
Center

Ft. Greene

363

Ranger
Station

Fort
Muhlenberg

Rd.

County Line Rd.

Outer Line Dr.

N. Gulph Rd.

422

ngton

National
Memorial
Arch

Thomas Rd.

Richards Rd.

76

Wayne's Woods
Picnic Area

Pennsylvania
Columns

Wayne
Statue

Glen Hardie Rd.

Baptist Rd.

Trout Ck.

Walker Rd.

252

0          1/2          miles 1

0          1/2          1 km

# Museums and Historic Sites

The following are just some of the points of interest found in the area covered by these rides. Many more buildings listed on the National Register of Historic Places (NRHP), museums, and Historic Districts are scattered throughout the region.

- Boyertown Museum of Historic Vehicles (Boyertown) 215-367-2090.
- Barns-Brinton House (Chadds Ford) 215-388-7376.
- Brandywine Battlefield State Park (Chadds Ford) 215-459-3342.
- Brandywine River Museum (Chadds Ford) 215-459-1900.
- Daniel Boone Homestead (Birdsboro) 215-582-4900.
- Historic Lancaster Walking Tour (Lancaster).
- Hopewell Furnace National Historic Site (Birdsboro area) 215-345-02120.
- James A. Michener Museum (Doylestown) 215-340-9800.
- Mercer Museum of Bucks County Historical Society (Doylestown) 215-345-0210.
- Lumberville NRHP Historic District (Bucks County).
- Pennsylvania Farm Museum of Landis Valley (Lancaster area) 717-569-0401.
- Railroad Museum of Pennsylvania (Strasburg) 717-687-8628.
- Valley Forge National Historical Society Museum (Valley Forge).
- Washington Crossing Historic Park (New Hope area) 215-493-4076.

# Cycling Information

Bicycle riding in the city and in the country is fun and will be safer when common sense and basic safety rules are followed. Knowing the rules of the road, developing good riding skills, maintaining a properly equipped bicycle, and matching a route to your fitness and skill level will add up to many miles of pleasurable cycle touring. Most of the following safety tips and graphics are reprinted with permission from city of Portland and city of Eugene, Oregon, publications.

## Safety tips

*In general:*
- **Be predictable.** Ride so drivers can see you and predict your movements. The rules in the driver's manual also apply to bicyclists.
- **Be alert.** Ride defensively and expect the unexpected. No matter who is at fault in an accident, the bicyclist loses.
- **Be equipped.** You will ride easier and safer if you and your bike have proper equipment.
- **Wear a helmet.** A hard shell helmet, meeting ANSI or Snell performance standards, is an essential element in your safety program.

*Country riding:*
- Ride single file and keep to the right when vehicles are approaching from behind and on sections of road with poor visibility.
- Slow down for gravel, sand, wet leaves, potholes, and other poor pavement conditions.
- Watch for dogs - dismount and place your bike between you and the dog if necessary.
- Be prepared for the air turbulence caused by fast-moving vehicles or large trucks.
- Treat railroad crossings with respect. Cross perpendicular to the tracks and assure yourself that it is clear and safe before making the crossing.

*In traffic:*

There are both commonsense and legal rules to follow when you are riding your bike in traffic. The following are some basic guidelines for safe cycling.

**Obey traffic signs, signals, and laws.** Bicyclists must ride like motorists if they are to be taken seriously by motorists.

**Never ride against traffic.** Motorists are not looking for bicyclists riding against traffic on the wrong side of the road.

**Scan the road around you.** Keep your eyes roving constantly for cars, pebbles, grates, etc. Learn to look back over your shoulder without swerving.

**Use a bike route.** Use bike lanes when you can. If a bike lane is not close by, keep up with traffic on narrow, busy streets or find a quieter street.

**Do not pass on the right.** On streets without bike lanes, do not overtake an automobile when approaching an intersection or when the automobile is signalling for a turn.

**Follow lane markings.** Do not turn left from the right lane. Do not go straight in a lane marked for right turn only.

**Observe dismount signs.** Where requested, dismount and walk your bike.

**Choose the best way to turn left.** Either signal, move into the left lane, and turn left, or ride straight to the far crosswalk, and walk your bike across.

**Ride in the middle of the lane in slow traffic.** Get in the middle of the lane at busy intersections and when you are moving at the same speed as traffic.

**You may leave a bike lane.** When hazards or obstructions block a bike lane or you are afraid a motorist might turn across your path, you may merge into the adjacent auto lane for safety.

**Use lights at night.** The law requires a strong headlight and rear reflector or taillight at night or when visibility is poor. Wear light-colored clothes with reflective tape for extra protection.

**Ride on sidewalks only where permitted.** Pedestrians have the right of way. Give them audible warning when you pass. Use extra caution when crossing driveways and intersections.

**Ride with both hands ready to brake.** Be prepared for quick stops and in rain allow three times the normal braking distance.

**Use hand signals.** Hand signals tell motorists what you intend to do. Signal as a matter of law, of courtesy, and of self-protection.

# Bicycle maintenance

Your bicycle requires periodic inspection and maintenance to keep it running reliably and safely. Several good books are available at bike shops, bookstores, and libraries, and bicycle maintenance and repair classes are sometimes offered through cities and schools.

Here are just a few maintenance pointers:
- Regularly lubricate your bike with the correct type of lubricant.
- Brakes should be checked and adjusted if necessary. Brake shoes should be about one-eighth inch from the rim.
- The chain should be lubricated and clean, and the gears properly adjusted.
- Tires should be fully inflated.
- The frame and attachments should be tight.
- Seat and handlebars should be adjusted correctly for you.

# Equipment

Since most of the routes in this book will lead you some distance from home, it is wise to carry a basic tool kit with you whenever you are on your bike. Your tool kit should include the following items:
- tire repair kit
- tire irons
- pump
- tube valve tool (if not part of valve cap)
- small crescent wrench
- screwdriver

In addition, it may be useful to have:
- spoke wrench
- pliers
- oil
- tape
- allen wrenches
- freewheel remover

Spare parts that can come in handy include:
- cables for derailleur and brakes
- tube
- brake shoes (2)
- spokes (3)

Almost all of these tools and parts will fit into a small seat or handlebar bag, and with them you can tackle just about any problem not requiring a bicycle shop or expert attention.

# Clothing

Wearing the right clothes and being prepared for adverse weather conditions will allow you to pedal merrily through varying weather patterns. Consider including these items in your riding wardrobe:

- a hat (in addition to your helmet)
- rain jacket or cape
- rain pants
- pant leg clips
- riding gloves
- sunglasses
- thermal tights and shirt
- riding shorts
- additional layers of clothing

# Fitness

One of the most pleasant side effects of touring by cycle or by foot is, of course, the opportunity to raise your general level of fitness. It is recommended that you get a physical examination and discuss a fitness program and activity with your doctor. For the casual daytripper and serious athlete alike, exercise should not be debilitating. Pace yourself, enjoy your activity, and plan your outings to accommodate your fitness level.

*Tips:*

- Go slowly at first; be patient; and always warm up before a session and cool down afterward.

- Progress at your own rate and try to infuse a long-term and consistent outlook into your activity.

- Look for variety in your exercise – both in activity and location.

- Develop a total fitness program that targets strength, aerobic capacity, and flexibility.

- Measure the amount of exercise you are getting in terms of time and intensity rather than just miles covered.

- Learn to pace yourself so that your energy resources are parceled out evenly over the course of the activity you have planned.

- Invest in clothing and equipment that matches your intensity and seriousness and that adds to your comfort and enjoyment of the activity.

# Calorie charts

These are some very approximate figures for calculating calories burned during different types of activities. The numbers inside the grey shaded area show the calories burned per minute for that activity.

## Walking

| Speed | Body Weight | | |
|-------|-------------|-----------|-----------|
| (mph) | 120 lbs. | 160 lbs. | 200 lbs. |
| 2 | 3 | 4 | 4 |
| 3 | 4 | 5 | 6 |
| 4 | 5 | 6 | 8 |
| 5 | 8 | 10 | 13 |

## Running

| Pace | Body Weight | | |
|------------|-------------|-----------|-----------|
| (min./mi.) | 120 lbs. | 160 lbs. | 200 lbs. |
| 11:30 | 7 | 10 | 12 |
| 9:00 | 10 | 14 | 18 |
| 8:00 | 11 | 15 | 19 |
| 7:00 | 12 | 16 | 21 |
| 6:00 | 14 | 18 | 23 |

## Cycling

| Speed (mph) | Calories per minute |
|-------------|---------------------|
| 5 | 2 |
| 10 | 5 |
| 15 | 10 |
| 20 | 17 |

# Route Consultants

### William Kelly

Bill and his wife Fay, pictured on this guide's front cover, moved to Chester County and have easy access to what they consider some of the best cycling roads in the country. They ride with the Brandywine Bicycle Club and regularly undertake long-distance tours.

### George Retseck

George rides extensively in the Bucks County area of southeastern Pennsylvania. He is a member of the Central Bucks Bicycle Club. He and his wife Pam have toured both in the U.S. and in Europe.

### William Hoffman

Bill is an active member of the Lancaster Bicycle Club and the League of American Wheelmen. He rides over 8000 miles a year and has completed many long-distance tours. He wrote Going Dutch, a general purpose guide book to southeastern Pennsylvania (see Around SE Pennsylvania).

# More Cycling Guides from Terragraphics

### Touring New England by Bicycle

New England has long been a favorite destination for a cycling vacation. This guide describes one- to five-day loops throughout the region for all levels of cyclists. Complete information, from spectacular 3-D topographic maps to mileage logs to accommodations, is presented for each route. Whether you are looking for a casual one-day jaunt or an inn-to-inn odyssey on the picturesque backroads of New England, you'll find rides that have been carefully planned by cyclists who have spent years touring here.
$10.95          ISBN 0-944376-08-8

### Touring the Washington D.C. Area by Bicycle

From the eastern shore of Chesapeake Bay to the Blue Ridge Mountains, the countryside surrounding our nation's capital offers cyclists a wide variety of terrain and landscapes. Thirty-three loop rides are described in detail, and hundreds of miles of good cycling roads are shown on topographic maps. You'll find routes that explore D.C.'s monuments, some off-road urban trails, many country backroads, and even mountain parkways.
$10.95          ISBN 0-944376-07-X

### Touring California's Wine Country by Bicycle

These California regions are known worldwide for the quality and variety of their wines. The 34 routes in this guidebook take into account wine-tasting opportunities, enjoying the countryside, and getting a good workout. Features rides in Napa, Sonoma, Sierra Foothill, Central Valley, and Coast regions.
$10.95          ISBN 0-944376-06-1